ALSO BY

LAURENT GAUDÉ

Hear Our Defeats

OUR EUROPE

Laurent Gaudé

OUR EUROPE
Banquet of Nations

*Translated from the French
by Alison Anderson*

Europa
editions

Europa Editions
8 Blackstock Mews
London N4 2BT
www.europaeditions.co.uk

Copyright © 2019 by Actes Sud
First Publication 2019 by Europa Editions

Translation by Alison Anderson
Original title: *Nous, l'Europe. Banquet des peuples*
Translation copyright © 2019 by Europa Editions

A catalogue record fro this title is available from the British Library
ISBN 978-1-78770-208-0

Gaudé, Laurent
Our Europe

Book design by Emanuele Ragnisco
www.mekkanografici.com

Prepress by Grafica Punto Print – Rome

Printed and bound in Great Britain by Clays Ltd, Elcograf S.p.A.

CONTENTS

OUR EUROPE

For some time now, Europe seems to have forgotten that it is the daughter of epics and utopia. It has been drained by its inability to remind its citizens of this. Too distant, disembodied, the concept often arouses nothing more than disillusioned boredom. And yet, the history of Europe is one of constant upheaval. So much fire and death; inventions and art, too. Literature, perhaps, can remind us of this: that the European story is one of muscles, vigor, passion, anger, and joy. Words of literature, perhaps, can restore conviction and momentum, which make everything possible, to the heart of the story.

Who are we? Which past have we inherited? What trials have we endured? What crimes have we committed, what utopias believed in? What do we want? Our continent has invented nightmares, made its own populations weep, but it was also the birthplace of an enlightenment that shone on the entire world. It is this contradiction that makes us who we are. We are nations of suffering, who have been intermingled for so long—in rivalry, trade, death, and desire, peoples so different that our decision to unite in a common assembly is an event unprecedented in history. In what other era, what other place, have we witnessed any such political adventure: twenty-eight countries deciding to host a great banquet of nations?

So many of those who came before us would be stunned to see the territory we have built. I am referring to the millions of men and women, our parents, grandparents, ancestors, who bore in their flesh the painful experience of borders. There are many who fled, leaving everything behind in the middle of the night, individuals thrown by History from one country into another. There are many of these border individuals, who take their country with them wherever they go. They have come to constitute a vast nation, speaking several languages and sharing memories of faraway traditions, and they know what upheaval means. Perhaps they constitute the true European model: a tormented people looking for a response to the harassment of History, and who have found it in the humanism they use as a compass in their wanderings.

Why did our countries decide to create this community of Entente? For the sake of peace. And besides peace? For prosperity. And besides prosperity? Was it to regain possession of those old demons of nations: competition, and the desire for domination? Is there no way to build Europe other than as a *translatio imperii*? After a period of waning influence, have the countries of Europe found—through the construction of Europe—a political structure which will grant them greater influence, in order to compete with the greatest, and "regain their rank"? We deserve the loftiest dreams, the maddest passions. We deserve to name the impossible and to work toward making it happen.

The past has shown us that only very rarely have we been able to come up with a plan other than domination. And yet, European integration will only have meaning if it is also an opportunity to come up with a new aim for civilization. Not to reign anymore—but to create, fully autonomously, the contours of an enlightened territory. And to be—why not?—a laboratory for dialogue between nations. For we must not delude ourselves: in the future, other regions of the planet will decide to unite. In the future, the contour of nations will be ever hazier. The planetary stakes of trade, the flow of information, the environment, energy, and our relationship with the animal world are all driving us toward this international dialogue. If we only evaluate our relation to raw materials on a nation-by-nation basis, this means evaluating them in conditions that lead to war. We know this, we have tested it so many times. Europe—with its slowness, debates, the constant necessity of coming to an agreement, its art of compromise to avoid paralysis, is the laboratory for what, increasingly often, humankind will have to do when they seek to reflect on the scale of the Earth and its ecosystem. In the future, we will have to engage in constant dialogue with all five continents. In the future, we will have to learn to foster a sense of belonging more all-encompassing than the one that ties us to our countries.

Everything dies. Perhaps someday we will say that we

were born in a world that is now buried. The civilizations of the Entente are fragile. They always have been. For a long time my generation took this Europe for granted, that it would remain the fixed framework of our lives, and now we are astonished to discover that our generation may be the one that will bury that Europe or, at least, the one that will see the first signs of its demise. Those who, like me, believe in this venture, will be to blame if we give way to the countervailing discourse. The point is not to deny the frustration, anger, or dissatisfaction. I too have felt these emotions—and often. But I want to distinguish between the anger that can be transformed into political struggle and the negation on principle of the great groundswell which, for over fifty years, has been building a country that is greater than our twenty-eight nations.

Our Europe was born of this desire: to tell our shared epic tale, and to do so with passion. As I am putting the finishing touches on this text, I realize it is in fact unfinished. Not that I have left the project I set myself incomplete, but because it suffers from the fact it is one voice when I would have liked for it to be many. All through its composition my constant concern has been to leave the story open as much as possible to the realities of neighboring European countries, and yet, alas . . . all through my work I have been forced to acknowledge how little I know about the history and geography of the twenty-seven other countries, and that, although it is not what I want, this story will remain one written by a Frenchman. I came to understand how much ground would have to be covered for us to have a common cultural core. In short, if *Our Europe* is an unfinished poem, it is because it is waiting for other voices—from Italy, Germany, Poland, Spain, and the others . . . so that one day, perhaps, a great text will be born, nourished by several flames that will share their light, their impressions, and their riches.

Until that day comes, I will continue to wander through my Europe. As I do so I will be thinking about this new sense of belonging that still has to take root and grow so that one day, when someone asks, "Who are you?" it will seem natural to reply using this one simple word that explains everything—both the turmoil of the past and the hope for the future: "I am European."

To the men and women who, immersed in the upheavals of History, said the word "Europe," with passion.

I
SO OLD SO YOUNG

Are we old?

Are we young?

How old are we, exactly?

Sometimes we're old people,

Sometimes slender youth,

We are the heirs to amassing years.

A long fossilization of languages, of cultures,

Successive deposits of so many past lives—mingled, enriched, superimposed,

Layers of war,

Of trade,

Of exchange,

Of conquest.

We are the sons and daughters of the sedimentation of centuries.

How old are we, exactly?

The borders have shifted,

Countries have expanded,

Empires, fallen.

A long river of History runs through us and gives us the density of time.

Perhaps this is what we are: old children,

Alliance of fatigue and enthusiasm.
Who can tell the exact date of our birth?

We have to dig into the 19th century.
The guts of modernity,
Bolts, hammers and fever,
We are made of the same flesh, the same nervousness.
Century of conquests and sweat,
Of progress and exploitation.
We have to dig into the 19th century, because it is like
    us:
It invented too fast,
Thought too deeply.
We have to plunge into its dirty belly,
Smell its factory armpits,
Listen to its voice, hoarse from shouting so long on the bar-
    ricades.
The 19th century, because it is the century of dizziness and
    hunger,
Tilting between two worlds,
Tottering before so much novelty and rumbling.
What is our date of birth?
We have to decide, so let me say it:
Palermo, January 12, 1848.
Something yearns for birth on that long-ago day,
Something growing,
Until it blows the old monarchies to smithereens.
Something will come to life
And it will be red and puling.
It will smell of viscera and sweat, but it's new.

Palermo is rising up
The first city to call for the Spring of Nations.

We were born of utopia and discontent.
Listen to the philosophers, agitators, and revolutionaries as
    they go from one capital to the next.
The insurrection is rumbling.
It erupts in Sicily,
Continues in Paris,
And from there, rebounds to every capital.
New words on people's lips,
Let's be done with empires,
Words passed around in secret
In private, in clandestine meetings,
"Nationalism,"
"Independence, unity, and freedom."
And all of a sudden, the crowd takes up those words,
In Milan,
In Berlin,
In Paris,
They want to overthrow the old world,
The world of the Vienna Congress that restored the monar-
    chies.
They want to throw off Metternich's policies
That chose order over freedom.
Countries want new names:
"Italy,"
"Germany,"
Nothing can stop the people once they catch the spirit of
    philosophers.

They want no more of that restored, established, arrogant
Europe.
The one that belongs to the Bourbons, Habsburgs,
Hohenzollern.
Europe has held banquets for some time now,
And we were born of their murmuring,
Of the passion slipped into words whispered low, but
yearning to be shouted loud.
1848 is our date of birth,
And that makes us children of the barricades,
Born in a muddle of wardrobes, carts, barrels, palisades,
and rifles . . .
Push again,
It has to come out
Never mind if it cries.
Europe rises in those days of 1848,
The Europe of Mazzini,
Of Friedrich Hecker and Gustav Struve,
Of Garibaldi,
Of Lajos Kossuth,
Of Ludwik Mierosławski and Ledru-Rollin,
A Europe of nations because, back then, nation would
mean emancipation,
The end of old kings dressed like dolls in toy carriages.
A nation is a people united around a language,
A culture,
And the poets give words to this rumbling anger,
Sándor Petőfi, Lamartine, Victor Hugo.
Even Verdi becomes a country's name.
Romanticism has conquered Europe,

And it carries the energy of rebellion within: Youth! Youth!
Are we old?
Not anymore.
Look: Europe is awakening and shaking its back.
It has a lovely rumpled face
And the hunger of a newborn child.

A generation is on its feet.
Universal suffrage,
Freedom of the press,
Votes for women,
A sovereign nation, no longer obeying sovereigns,
Ideas that run from mouth to mouth,
And everyone cherishes them like a precious treasure.
They will still be there,
Twenty years later,
When the states are born.
Europe is taking shape, seeking its identity,
Wondering what it wants,
It shakes off royalty,
Turns to it again.
Rejects it again.
They've thought and dreamt and fought
From Berlin to Paris,
Vienna to Geneva.
Sought exile in London or Brussels,
Came home to their country,
Only to flee once more.
How many went with Mazzini, the members of the
    Giovane Italia?

One hundred?
A thousand?
Giovane Europa,
Giovane Germania,
Giovane Ungheria,
Giovane Polonia,
Giovane is the name of national awakening.
Youth!
Youth!
That is all we need,
Three hundred young people,
Perhaps five,
In every country of our Union,
To revive the Carbonari tradition,
And think not of what is possible,
But of the dream,
To turn their eyes toward the unknown,
To try to name it,
Then wield it.
Giovane Europa,
Five hundred young people in every country,
Several thousand souls,
But it's a movement,
Young people talking, uniting, sharing, hoping for more.
That is all we need,
Their desire stubborn,
Ambitious,
Inspiring.
Giovane Europa,
The countries appear, one after the other,

Belgium, Italy, and Germany.
Don't mistake them for celebrated births,
Don't think anyone marveled at their size, or the delicacy
    of their infant features.
Nothing is easy between people and borders.
These newborn babies want us to make room for them,
When no one wants to move.
So, everything begins to tremble.
We tear our hair,
Joyfully annex one another,
And ardently fight.

Do you think we are living in troubled times?
You feel the breath of history and are afraid,
And wonder what fever afflicts our era?
Does it frighten you to see, suddenly, the restless mood of
    nations?
Think of Victor Hugo, in exile.
Think of Garibaldi crossing the Atlantic, fighting in Brazil,
    Argentina, Uruguay,
The "Hero of the Two Worlds" exhausted by a life of
    wounds.
He persists into old age, still fighting in Dijon at the age of
    sixty-four, when he can hardly mount his horse.
There are no peaceful times.
Think of Friedrich Hecker,
Who joins the 1848 revolution in the streets of Baden, then
    flees to America and fights for the Union in the Civil
    War . . .
Think of all those we called the Forty-Eighters,

Who lived through the Spring of Nations,
Then, the return of kings,
And finally, true independence,
All in one lifetime.
Think of the war of the "Terrible Year"[1]
Europe asunder, in search of its soul.
Nice and Savoy change hands,
Alsace and Lorraine, too.
Europe longs for borders but cannot find them,
And so rushes into war,
Signs treaties, agreements, betrayals,
Beneath the watchful gaze of the Sultan and the Tsar.

Europe produces,
Builds,
Fights,
But also starves to death,
Takes the road to exile.
The Irish die in their thousands, and Queen Victoria stands
    unblinking.
The first Italians set sail for America, and never know that
    Emma Lazarus's[2] colossus will watch them go by for
    decades.
Oh, these lands of turmoil . . .
So many events,
So much unrest,

[1] "L'année terrible," a poem by Victor Hugo, written in 1871.
[2] "The New Colossus," a poem by Emma Lazarus, written in 1883.

So many lives destroyed . . .

And you think we live in troubled times?

Has any generation ever known less danger, greater calm?

The two centuries before us were nothing but striving, fever, onslaught, and revolution.

The centuries before us were ogres, devouring courage and genius, whole lives at a time.

And here we are,

With these words handed down to us:

"Nation," "Equality," "Freedom,"

And we contemplate them wearily.

For we have long become citizens of boredom.

Oh, youth!

Youth!

We need your swift awakening.

II
COAL LIGHT

Now born, we must eat.

Heat, friction, smoke,

Will make us grow.

We shall devour forests, entire countrysides,

Stuff ourselves with the genius of humankind and its labor,

Engulf what is old and then rebuild.

A great blast of steam.

Our world appears in stunned silence.

Before this awe-inspiring sleight of hand.

Listen carefully,

Can you hear that sound of pressure like we've never known?

See the surprise on the faces of the crowd,

The very image of Progress.

Nothing will ever be as it was,

The world will never return,

There is a machine,

Shining new,

Foretelling lives we cannot even imagine.

Spit, smoke,

Ramp up the pace, hotter, faster!

Tirelessly,

We will never tire again . . .
Well-oiled piston, endlessly.
Combustion, more, more!
Ramp up the pace, hotter!
Faster,
More, more!

Witnesses are ecstatic,
But the race has just begun.
We have to dig into the 19th century
Because in its guts lies our face.
We were born from this fertile womb
With its treasures and scowls,
Warmth and moisture.

It begins here,
With *The Rocket*,
On September 15, 1830.
The first passenger locomotive appears.
Running from Liverpool to Manchester,
At more than twenty-five miles an hour
And the feat amazes us all.
Stephenson rejoices.
Does he sense that Europe will soon pulse with tracks?
It has begun with his invention,
Or any of those suddenly appearing.
A succession of ingenious changes, advances, modifica-
    tions,
Patents applied for, to improve on previous inventions,
Or pillage them.

New things appear
Some a bit crazy,
A bit cumbersome,
Making strange sounds,
New things their inventors demonstrate with sweeping ges-
    tures
To a skeptical audience.
New things, ever increasing in number.
Prolific heart,
Gears,
Motors,
Pistons.
An unbelievable revolution.
Power looms.
Daguerreotypes.
Steam engines.
Dynamos.
Listen to these gentlemen—Watt, Gramme, Benz, Bell,
    Daguerre, Morse, Nobel, and Colt—explaining the
    multiple uses for their inventions.
And they will work.
Everything will work.
Everything heating, and running, fast.

Oh yes, everything is expanding quickly now,
And our robust body feels strong enough to lift the earth
To kiss the sky,
To dazzle the night.
Everyone's looking, everywhere,
As it all gets carried away.

Steam, sweat,
It's heating up!
Steam, sweat,
Faster!
Europe's nails are black and its cheeks are red.
It's heating up!
The race has begun and continues on.
Soon we'll have trams, cars, the underground . . .
Steam, sweat,
Faster, harder!
Gee up, machine!
Gee up, no more stopping, ever!
It's all heating up,
Intensifying.
Coal reigns over a world hungering to try, to seek, to improve.
Humanity plunges headlong into production.
It all starts here,
With the new, repetitive, mechanical sound of the looms,
It leaves them stunned, those girls who become the first
    workers, now stepping somewhat fearfully into these
    vast mills, and wondering what their new job will be,
Unaware that from now on they will live in thrall to
    rhythm, morning to night.
It begins here—
Not Europe,
Which goes back further—
No,
Our world,
Because the blast of steam leads straight to us.
We were born of it.

Children of industrialization
And the reign of machines,
That moment when it all accelerated and European man
    saw the world was a juicy fruit ripe for the plucking.
And in this staccato noise from the warehouses of London,
    Paris, and Berlin,
One word, over and over, three revolutions per second,
Listen:
Competition, competition, competition.

Gee up!
We have to go faster,
Farther.
Our eyes, always, riveted on our neighbors.
Keep the advantage,
Don't get left behind.
You have to be the one who enlightens, influences, domi-
    nates.
Gee up!
The only rule is rivalry.
Have you heard of free trade?
We have never stopped believing in it,
Free trade until it overheats.
We are the children of rivalry.
It is as old as nations
Because from the start, our countries have loved nothing
    better than a rival outdone.

*The Great Exhibition of the Works of Industry of All
    Nations,*

Come in,
You'll be amazed!
It's all ready.
Come to Joseph Paxton's Crystal Palace!
Four hundred tons of glass in Hyde Park,
Four thousand tons of metal,
A beautiful sharp building over six million visitors will rush
    to see
From May to October, 1851,
Six million for this first universal exhibition,
That's a lot of people,
That's a lot of oohs and aahs!
Of amazement,
Wonder,
Incredulity.
So many eyes like saucers,
Gaping mouths,
Ladies dazzled
And gentlemen turned engineers
Trying to explain the whys and wherefores to their partners,
And the ladies, not knowing what to say, intersperse their
    visit with "Oh, really? . . . As many as that?"

Prince Albert has had an extraordinary idea:
At the entrance
He has installed a twenty-four-ton block of solid coal,
Just like that.
Monumental.
Twenty-four tons of coal,
And it's true:

England knows its power comes from coal,
Knows that with coal, it will give birth to tomorrow's
    world,
Knows that this word,
"Coal,"
Will place its signature upon the century.
Always the same old story:
An era chooses its raw material and gorges itself.
Europe came to be, with coal.
The cities where we live,
The wars we fought,
The objects trailing us through life,
Long bore that name: coal.
The whole world wants it.
So they must dig.
Black faces,
In England, Wales, Wallonia, or Poland.
From father to son,
Grandfather to grandson.
Black faces from woman to woman, too.
Black from rubbing dirty linen,
From emptying the bowl at the foot of the bed where the
    husband spits and coughs at night.
Black faces by entire families.
Factories running,
Machines wolfing down charcoal,
Machines devouring lives.
A race of proud lads.
Going down the mine, coming back into the light,
An entire life like that

At the foot of these slag heaps, mushrooming mausolea for
the men who cough.
You have to work the coal, and it never stops, because
down the pit, there are no seasons.
And in the end, you die of firedamp or you die coughing,
it all depends.
Black faces, broken faces.
A long lineage, wearing thin.
Dead, alive, you end up not really knowing anymore.
An entire life in the bowels of the earth so others may live
in the light.
That word,
Coal,
To tell how the world has changed.
The plow fading away, with its old animal slowness,
Replaced by nervous little carts screeching like teeth back
up to the daylight, laden with the sweat of men.

That's what Albert's block of coal is saying:
That in the Crystal Palace lie
Twenty-four tons of faith in the future,
Twenty-four tons of comfort and discovery to come.
And even more underground!
Thousands of hundreds of thousands of tons,
Inexhaustible seams of resources . . .
God save the Queen
Since He gave the English crown the right to be the first
producer of coal.
Albert does not know that a century later
From December 5th to 9th, 1952,

His great-grandchildren
Will cough like consumptives
Trapped in a great cloud of fog:
The Great Smog.
It's been bloody cold these last weeks of November.
Everyone wants heat.
The war's barely over,
The coal is bad quality
And there's not a puff of wind.
Five days of thick fog.
A yellow-black cloud, they call it.
The great machine is running out of steam.
For a century, they have pumped, extracted, burned, con-
    sumed
And suddenly in broad daylight cannot see six feet ahead.
The Great Smog,
One century later,
In response to the great block of twenty-four tons.
The machine wears down.
Overheating the cities!
Derailment,
Suffocation!
And when at last the smog disappears,
Swept by winds that took pity on humankind,
It will have poisoned over ten thousand Londoners
Who die within months from the air they breathed,
Purulent acute bronchitis,
Infected coughs, spitting up blood.
Does Albert hear them?
Has anyone thought of throwing a stone at the Albert

Hall to vent their anger at their coal-kindled suffocation?

No.

Because for the people of 1952 there is no link between the smog that paints the streets yellow and the beautiful Great Exhibition of 1851, which consecrated the values of trade and human ingenuity.

That is just what the *Great Exhibition* said,

With its fountain of crystal thirty feet high, enchanting the ladies:

Free trade is a pillar of modernity,

Trade among nations must produce wealth

And this wealth will flow to everyone,

Down to every last East End Oliver Twist.

It's just that the coal-blackened faces never saw a drop of that miracle flow

And nations were swayed by one thing only:

Competition,

And that alone.

My turn now.

We each get a turn.

Europe has a new game:

The procession of progress.

It's my turn now.

And it will be bigger, higher, more amazing!

We're getting busy in Paris,

We must be ready for 1855.

We're building the Palais de l'Industrie,

But since we're in France,

Mother of arts and weapons and all that,
The exhibition will feature artists, too.
"They didn't think about that, did they, those Brits!"
So we call on Courbet, Ingres, Delacroix:
Make it shiny!
My turn now.
No sooner has Paris finished than England wants to play
    again,
A nervous ping-pong between capitals.
1862, London,
1867, Paris, then Vienna, then Paris again.
Then, Brussels,
Let me play!
It's my turn!
Bigger, stronger!
Paris builds the Grand Palais,
Milan celebrates the opening of the Simplon Tunnel.
The train, yet again,
You can cross the Alps in a seat now.
Barcelona, the United States, Australia,
Now it's my turn.
Everyone wants to play.
Competition in every domain.
Paris is greediest of all,
They could practically hold a universal exhibition every
    year to make up for the affront of not being first.
We were born of those times, born of genius,
Frenzied activity,
Extreme competition,
Paternalistic patriotism.

Those years of soot-covered faces
And the hunger of jobless men.
We were born of great rivalry.
Every city wanted to reign.
Every city wanted to invite its neighbors to its own conse-
cration.
An Eiffel Tower was built
And an underground railway.
A Cirque d'Hiver was built
And everything is radiant.
Europe is moving quickly.
Overheating.
Going ever further,
To gain the upper hand,
Ever shinier,
What matters,
In Paris, London, and Berlin,
Is rivalry,
And it is ruthless.

Oh, the cities do change . . .
More than anything, perhaps,
We are the children of the monstrous expansion of cities,
They become a world,
They become light, a stage,
And unspeakable slums.
Imagine this:
The stinking neighborhoods of Paris,
The great covered markets reeking of meat and cold blood.
Imagine horses, everywhere,

Eighty thousand horses in Paris,
Manure piled high!
You need a lot of street sweepers and road workers . . .
Over six hundred, just to deal with the daily droppings.
Cities still smell of beasts,
But not for much longer.
People hope for cars,
And Haussmann is sharpening his pencils, to draw nice
 straight lines through the capital.
The Bretons are still pouring out of the Gare
 Montparnasse,
Kids still crowding into houses that smell of bad charcoal
And London stinks.
They've given a name to this bad smell:
The Great Stink.
The summer of 1858 is one long ordeal,
Sticky and smelly.
Everyone is suffocating, even in the lofty chambers of
 Westminster
And the Thames is nothing but a river of excrement:
Dead animals,
Offal from slaughterhouses,
Human shit,
And rubbish rotting in the heat.
London stinks
So they invent sewers.
Cities expand,
Swallow countrysides,
Absorb the fields around them, to create parks, or new
 neighborhoods,

They expand the center,
So many lives squeezed in there
Suddenly meeting,
Becoming neighbors.
So many lives learning to live on top of each other,
We already knew the jacqueries,
Angry crowds bristling with pitchforks and pickaxes;
Now we discover the barricades.
The avenues must be made wider, and Baron Haussmann
    sets to work, so the police can charge on horseback,
    restore order.
"The demolishing artist," he likes to call himself.
Make Paris a checkerboard,
Limit the labyrinthine districts of rabble,
Breeding grounds of troublemakers, maniacs you can't
    flush out,
"Decontamination" is the fashionable term in salons,
Along with "urbanism," still forming in people's minds . . .
The city is growing, drawing crowds of new lives,
More and more lives . . .
Jostling around the stations,
A medley of accents.
The cities become enormous.
The lucky ones work from dawn to dusk,
Others hold out their hands.
Look at Fernand Pelez's begging children,
Selling matches,
Mothers burdened with wee ones, their exhausted gazes.
Imagine the raw poverty of working-class neighborhoods,
    each helping the other with what little they've got

As they watch the carriages in the distance
Whose wheels on the cobbles make a sound of scorn.

Faster, harder!
Gee up, mare-machine!
More and more,
Into the ground!
The factories are running.
Looms,
Smelting furnaces,
Locomotives.
We've never heard such thunderous sounds.
And they consume the men . . .
The industrial revolution invented not only machines,
But anger and the proletariat.
It was all of an era:
Victor Hugo and Karl Marx,
The Great Famine in Ireland and *The Communist Manifesto*.
They all meet, debate, inflame the world of ideas,
Engels, Proudhon, Blanqui, Garibaldi.
All fugitives, in hiding, familiar with exile.
It does exist, a Europe where people flee in the middle of
     the night,
The Europe of communists,
Anarchists,
Nefarious thinkers
Who have decided their destiny is to strike a decisive blow
     against the old world.
And they speak every language,
Seek shelter under every roof,

Are worn down with prison stays and clandestine journeys.
Europe is rumbling
From hunger
And knows very well that what was born in this century
Feeds off one thing alone:
The labor of those who have nothing.

Faster, harder,
Stoke it, hotter!
Production, combustion,
More, more!
Gee up, you machinery, grinding the faceless masses,
Gee up, flat out, with your burning steam,
Everything is heating up, getting excited,
The electricity fairy has just decreed her reign.
Light in the streets,
In spirits,
Light everywhere!
Half a century of racing,
Of wonder,
Of invention,
Half a century of exploitation,
Of progress and regression,
Half a century of entire boatloads leaving Europe, bound
    for the New World.
Half a century of prosperity and poverty
Empires born and stock markets crashing.
Birth of the railways, crisscrossing Europe.
Reigning now over every route
But they will also bring on the crisis.

The Vienna Stock Exchange topples,[3]
Then, along with it, Paris and Berlin.
The cash is gone.
And it will go along, from now on:
From one crash to the next,
Overheating, collapsing,
The world turned manic depressive.
In one hand, electricity; in the other, absinthe.
Light and drunkenness
Toward the great black hole
We feel it coming
But cannot turn back.
We've headed that way for too long,
Toward that great black hole,
As if it were our fate.
Gee up!
Faster,
Harder,
Into the grave!
Drive,
Whip,
Sweat, steam,
It has to be hotter,
Even in the abyss!

[3] Vienna Stock Market crash of 1873.

III
THE WORLD DEVOURED

What we eat makes us what we are
And for centuries we have eaten the world.
Our countries have run the race
For raw materials.
To be the seller, not the buyer,
The one to choose, not to submit.
All decided in a matter of decades.
What did we do when we reigned?
We gorged ourselves.
And as our countries were so small,
We invented the Conference of Carving Up.
The model will be used again and again,
Adapted to every need:
Four or five men around a table,
A map spread before them,
Whiskey glasses and ashtrays—because nights of negotia-
    tion can be long,
And a ruler to draw lines across nations divided.
One for you,
One for me,
Cities,

Populations,
Entire civilizations,
One side or the other,
One for you,
One for me,
Depending on your mood and the balance of power.
They are all there, in Berlin in 1885: French, Italians,
  British, Spanish, Belgians, Danes, Dutch, Portuguese,
  Russians, Norwegians, Ottomans, Americans, and
  Austro-Hungarians
Staring at a huge dish:
Africa.
Bigger than their eyes, their mouths, their bellies,
But that doesn't matter,
They eat for more than themselves,
They eat for their children and grandchildren.
They eat for at least a century of colonization.
It's well worth sitting down at the table . . .
*"Any European power established on the coast can extend its
  domination inland until it meets a neighboring sphere of
  influence."*
That's the agreement at the conference in Berlin.
Can you imagine?
It leaves you with a lot of latitude, a concept like that.
We'll have the rivers!
Sail upstream as quickly as possible.
Hurry, before the others get there!
We'll have the trading posts along the riverbanks!
The rule is simple: as long as only Blacks are there, it's
  ours.

First come, first served.
Hurry!
Go get Livingstone and Stanley.
Oscar Baumann and Lenz,
Burton and Brazza,
Put on your pith helmets,
Pack your trunks,
There's no time to lose!
Go get Captains Binger and Gouraud,
Voulet and Chanoine,
Who'll kill everything in their path, even the French who
try to stop them.
Go on, quickly!
The race has begun.
We need everything: rubber, wood, precious gems, coffee,
chocolate, sugar, pepper, and all the new spices.
We need ivory for our billiard balls and piano keys.
Primary raw materials,
Secondary raw materials,
Luxury products to basic necessities.
All there in the African soil,
All there, in the Caribbean and South America,
Just get organized, and get there first.

Nations help themselves, individuals, too.
An entire country for a single man, you think that cannot
be?
You know who the Congo belongs to?
"Private Property of the King of the Belgians."
Léopold II,

Spit on his name,
With his fine beard
And his officer's nose.
No "Belgian colony,"
No,
"Property of the King."
Léopold II,
Spit on his name,
The Congo is his garden,
His playground.
And he doesn't like hands, Léopold,
Spit on his name,
At least not black hands
He must think they're not needed ...
So he has them chopped off
On a grand scale.
The African worker who doesn't bring back enough rub-
ber, or runs away,
All the lazy, resistant ones:
Punish them!
Always the same:
Chop! Chop!
You think that's monstrous?
And yet there are statues depicting Léopold II
Here and there
Spit on his name
Place du Trône in Brussels
Place Wiertz in Namur,
An avenue in Paris leading to the Place Rodin.
Léopold with his red hands,

On whom Mark Twain[4] spat, but it was not enough,
On whom Arthur Conan Doyle[5] spat, but it was not
    enough . . .
The Congo was his house,
Full stop.
His sphere of influence, so to speak.
There are others,
Zones for practicing massacre,
For exploiting human sweat.
Every country has its own.
Germany will cut its teeth on Namibia,
Sending Lothar von Trotha
        Spit on his name,
Because he put down the Boxer rebellion.
He knows how to crush people and they want him to do it
    again,
Since no one could give a damn.
Have done with the Hereros.
Lothar von Trotha,
        Spit on his name,
Will sign a *Vernichtungsbefehl*,
An order of extermination,
Sounds odd, don't you think?
Does it remind you of anything?
Vernichtungslager.
I tell you,
They're practicing in Namibia.

[4] *King Leopold's Soliloquy.*
[5] *The Crime of the Congo.*

And it is going well.
Lothar von Trotha,
  Spit on his name,
Has actually written:
"Within German borders, every armed Herero will be slain.
  I will accept no women or children either."
Does that remind you of anything?
Not a single one.
Not a single one must remain,
Wipe the place clean.
And Göring, that vile man,
Hermann Göring,
  Spit on his name,
Had a daddy,
Heinrich,
Who was posted to Namibia, too.
He must have told his son some pretty stories.
There is a link between the brutal crushing of Africa,
The voracious exploitation of its resources,
The permanent exercise of abuse,
Of authority,
Of cold arrogance,
And what comes next.
So many men, sent to that land like all-powerful dogs, got
  used to reigning like little tyrants,
To raping all they liked,
To killing with impunity,
To taking pleasure in being master.
So many men enslaving so many others
Seeing nothing the least bit wrong with it . . .

Vernichtung
The word is planted in the ground
And will keep on growing.

Zones of influence,
Do you know where they are?
In Indonesia and Surinam: the Netherlands.
In West Africa, Indochina, and North Africa: France.
In Angola: Portugal.
In Ethiopia: Italy
Mussolini puts Pietro Badoglio in charge of testing gas on
    the Negus's armies,
        Spit on his name, on both their names.
He takes Addis Ababa by covering the country with mus-
    tard clouds that kill indiscriminately: warriors,
Cattle,
Children.
Rodolfo Graziani,
        Spit on his name,
"Vice-Governor of Italian Cyrenaica,"
"Viceroy of Italian East Africa,"
Who does not have his equal when it comes to crushing
    rebels,
Gets the better of Omar al-Mukhtar, the Lion of the
    Desert,
And has him hanged like a common beggar.
An unjust death:
Graziani,
        Spit on his name,
Survives an assassination attempt in Addis Ababa.

Why does death not want him?
Is it afraid of dirtying its hands?
But it does take hundreds of Ethiopians, killed in
    reprisal.
There is a Europe of big wildcats,
In uniform,
Gazing out at African landscapes in the early morning,
Convinced they are serving the fatherland.
Franco,
        Spit on his name,
Will cut his teeth on Morocco.
Fighting the Moors in the Rif war,
Convinced, no doubt, that he is continuing the good works
    of Catholic Isabella.
And even those who are exemplary,
Even the great soldiers,
Like Gallieni,
Behave in the colonies like Old Man Whipper,
Bothered by the noise of natives.
Which goes to show there's no telling,
Who'll be wiser or bloodier,
The very structure of colonialism makes them ugly.
Gallieni arrives at Antananarivo
To "restore order."
So Madagascar bleeds.
People are shot without trial,
There are shows of force,
The rabble are killed for any vague desire,
And when calm returns,
When the island is dazed with slaughter,

Schools and infirmaries are built to care for the newly-
 orphaned children.
I tell you, Europe is practicing:
Oppression, without flinching.

IV
WE SHALL SLEEP NO MORE

When did Europe start losing sleep?
When did it start to listen more carefully?
When did it start to worry,
To be plagued by nightmares?
"There is less sleep in the world today."[6]
Listen to the voice of Stefan Zweig,
Son of a civilization soon to vanish.
The world no longer knows how to sleep,
Everything is turmoil, raw nerves, loud colors.
It trembles beneath painters' fingers.
Man is a blue horseman.
Die Brücke,
Der Blaue Reiter,
Uneasiness of forms.
Bodies twisting,
Mouths opened wide,
Spurts of red, green, sleepless blue,
Everything is anxious,
And the world, more and more, speaks in a regimental
    voice.

[6] *Die Schlaflose Welt* by Stefan Zweig.

Identity?
Qualified or unqualified, that's all.
Nationality?
Ally or enemy, nothing more.
Profession?
Soldier or worker, that will do.
A new era is getting ready
That doesn't care about fathers, brothers, lovers,
Doesn't care about feelings, handkerchiefs, promises of
    swift return.
It needs men, hordes of men.
They'll have to get used to being one among many,
In the factories
Or the military.
Troops, crowds, regiments.
The era of the little man is beginning,
The featureless little man
Like his neighbor in every way,
The little man who is great only through suffering
Through what he is capable of enduring.
That's what's needed.
It is time to be numerous
And disciplined.

It begins with the bell, in the villages,
Ringing the general mobilization
And it's chilling
That a feeble little sound
Can carry with it so much blood . . .
Then, the sound of horses at night on the cobbled roads

As the regiments head for the front
And you can't get over it, seeing so many sons go by,
So young, all of them,
So handsome in these nights of departure.
It continues in a hail of bullets,
Oh, yes, the bullets,
We were bound to get there.
The saber rattling,
The threats,
The curses,
Were all for this.
To mass the troops at the border
And inspect the regiments,
All for this.
Speed up production of shells
And write the scripts for battle,
All for this.
And finally, once they've puffed out their chests and
counted their troops,
It's time to tear each other apart,
So off they go.

Plant the crosses in these vast fields,
More,
Always more.
Plant the crosses,
Hang the plaques,
Put up the statues:
Died for France on the field of honor, glory to the home-
land and all of that . . .

Plant,
Plant,
We'll need so many
Because what's coming will be global . . .
They'll come from far away to die here.
Polish the coffins,
Dig the graves,
We'll need more than you could ever imagine.
Side by side,
Elbow to elbow.
Carve the names in the marble,
More names,
Unending lists of names.
And all the statues it will take,
The monuments,
The minutes of silence,
To pay tribute to those we've sacrificed.
All the shovelfuls it will take
To bury all the bodies the century's devoured.

And then it begins.
Never seen anything like it:
The shock of steel and soil,
A gale of metal tearing lives and trees apart,
Plowing the soil,
Searing daylight,
Deafening the night.
It begins with the cannonade and ends with the moans of
    the dying,
Sobs, murmurs, gurgling,

Little sounds of fear, exhaustion, almost animal distress.
In the infirmary tents, the blood is gushing,
Flowing everywhere,
Oozing,
You slip on the meat, there's so much of it.
You don't even clean between two bodies.
Amputating as quickly as possible.
They scream amid the odor of charred flesh
Before they pass out
Or die.
And the legs, the arms, the hands severed, still there in the
    surgeon's fingers
As he hesitates a moment,
Cannot fathom how much he has sawn off since morning,
And he stands there, paralyzed,
In a moment suspended his mind goes blank,
"Doctor?"
"Doctor?"
The nurse calls him, shakes him by the sleeve,
He must get a grip,
Others are groaning, waiting, their forces ebbing,
"Doctor?"
He suddenly awakens,
Again sees before him the suffering bodies,
Another wounded man is brought in,
Is placed upon the table,
Bleeding and screaming.
Nothing ever prepared him for so many garrots, so much
    amputation,
Nothing, ever,

And he does not know what he is becoming,
A doctor,
Or a guardian of Hell.
He doesn't know
But his hands move
And the wounded sob or pass out,
Sob or pass out,
Sob or pass out,
Oh God,
Where are you?
Sob or pass out . . .

The night is over
The cycle of day and night is over,
The heavy rest of peasants is over.
Over.
We can kill at any time
And if we're not killing, we're living in fear
And that keeps us awake.
We huddle in our holes,
We listen out,
We evacuate our fear in stomach cramps and smells of
    shit
And we pray,
Many of us pray,
Because that's all there is to do,
And never mind if the men on the other side are praying,
    too,
It's up to who prays loudest.

Our Father, who art in heaven, give us the strength to kill
Make us stronger than our enemies From the bottom of
the abyss we are so small And we cry day and night Lord
How could you possibly not hear Our Father who art in
heaven Make yourself deaf to our enemy even if they are
praying too They cannot pray as fervently as we can Our
Father deliver us from blood through victory Hail Mary
full of grace Hail all the saints provided they help me and
give me the strength to get up to run to shoot faster than
the one aiming at me Holy Mary Mother of God It's now
you have to save us Now because death is devouring us
Death is greedy Holy Mother of corpses And you alone
can save us Our Father who art in heaven or elsewhere
Have mercy Wherever you are Mercy

Slaughter,
Slaughter.
Never has the earth smelled of so much blood.
The men in Liège will fall
And everything starts again.
The Wallon city is attacked, resists, then eventually gives
    in.
"Those who died for the world, there in Liège"[7]
Merely repelled the slaughter for a few days.
But it's coming, taking great strides toward us.
In one day,[8]
Only twenty-five days after the start of the war,

---

[7] "Ceux de Liège," a poem by Émile Verhaeren, published in 1916.
[8] August 22, 1914.

Twenty-five thousand French soldiers die
Not far from Charleroi,
In a blaze of steel.
Who can sleep after this?
Who can dream after surviving this?
A continent hurls itself into the abyss.
Slaughter,
Slaughter.
Nation-states run amok,
The Moloch of European youth.
A feeding frenzy of flesh,
An orgy of lives,
Dying by the armful,
At the age of eighteen or twenty,
With lives ahead of them untouched by even a fingertip
Because they will die virgins,
Some even beardless.
Who can sleep in Belgium?
In the Somme,
The Ardennes,
Or on the Eastern front?
Who can sleep in the trenches?
Steel falling from the heavens,
Shells by the thousands,
Disfiguring the earth at a factory tempo,
Driving men mad,
Hail,
Storm,
Flood,
There are no more words for the unceasing pounding,

Which simply wants to crush life,
All life.

Ypres is the name of our great cough.
It should have been Bolimóv,
When the general August von Mackensen
      Spit on his name,
Ordered eighteen thousand shells of xylyl bromide to be
    fired at the Russian lines,
But History took no interest in that day.
The air was too cold for the gas
And the winds scattered the clouds.
History is waiting for Ypres, which comes less than three
    months later.
April 22, 1915,
The Germans try again
And this time it works.
The mustard gas spreads
Thick, oily, orange
And soon it gets its name: *yperite*.
From the place where it was used—not for the first time—
But where, for the first time, it was used to satisfaction.
Coughing, vomiting, dying.
The gas would darken the front.
Coughing, vomiting, dying.
They did suspect it was a weapon with prospects . . .
Ask Lothar von Trotha, who tried in Namibia,
Ask Pietro Badoglio, who tried in Ethiopia,
Ask the English, with their picric acid in the Boer war,
They could tell it would kill en masse,

But never in Europe.
Ypres is the name of the woundless dead, their eyes wide
   open,
Trying to breathe through a mouth squeezed closed.
The more they breathe, the more they die,
And once they know they're dying, the more they want to
   breathe.
Ypres is science in the service of death,
Of all those German, English, French chemists,
Who ran trials, and tried to improve their products—
   killing rats and monkeys, clocking the time it took.
Ypres is the name of a blister on the face of humanity.

Europe becomes an open land,
With its trenches,
Its craters,
Its ruined towns.
Europe becomes a land of unknown soldiers,
Of whom only bits are found,
Or nothing at all.
We just know they were there, at the heart of the blast,
In hell,
And now they are no more.
John Kipling, Rudyard's son, was killed at Loos-en-
   Gohelle, his first time at the front.
"You'll be a Man, my son!"[9]
Only just eighteen.

[9] "If," poem by Rudyard Kipling.

He was nearsighted, was John,
And had been declared unfit for service,
But he begged his father to help,
And Rudyard Kipling had a word with a few friends.
His son was able to enlist and went to die on land that
    would not even give him back.
John and so many others,
Who did not have famous fathers,
Who had flat feet,
Or a lisp,
Or had never left their village,
Had never been separated from their families,
And they, all of them,
Big, rather boastful young men,
A bit stupid,
Some of them still virgins,
All of them,
English,
Canadian,
Come to die so soon.
Trench fodder.
That'll make a few crosses in the military graveyards,
Lots of pretty crosses all in a row,
Whole nations of crosses,
And Kipling the elder will search the land around Loos.
Until his own day to die,
Organizing searches for his son's remains.
He is crazed with grief,
And stubbornly scratches the earth:
"Give me back my son . . . "

He will ask the same questions a thousand times,
Will come back again and again,
The old Greek gesture of wanting a burial.
Kipling,
An old man adrift in his sin,
Half King Lear,
Half Antigone
Unable to bear that word of torture a moment more,
"Unknown,"
For none of them were "unknown."
They all had names,
Families.
They had friends, plans, humor, and talent.
They wrote letters,
Played cards,
Counted the days.
Unknown, no.
And so Kipling came up with a formula:
"Known unto God"
And perhaps that brought him some comfort,
Known unto God,
Unto God alone but unto God all the same.
Rudyard can tell himself that God, at least, can see his son.
Knows where he lies,
Can name him and take him in.
He must have seen his fill, God . . .
He must have been stunned by those long columns of
     young men coming toward him,
French, German, English, Irish, Canadian, Senegalese,
     Tunisian, Moroccan, Vietnamese, Belgian, Russian,

He must have been aghast,
So many languages,
So many crushed faces,
And then one day Kipling begins to weep again,
Because he senses that *"known unto God"* will no longer
    bring any consolation.
And with him all the mothers in Europe are weeping
But it makes no sound
For they do so quietly,
At night,
Biting their pillow,
Or whenever they walk past the monument to the dead
    that has just been built on the square outside the town
    hall,
And where their child's name has been carved.
It startles them,
That name,
Cherished, kissed, prayed for so many times,
That name
Carved in death.
They weep and spit, those mothers,
Because they feel like being angry,
And they are right.
No more sleep,
No more laughter,
They will be like millions of other mothers all over Europe,
Amputated,
Wondering what could have possibly led to such a feeding
    frenzy,
Hardly remembering what joy once felt like,

And wondering,
On nights when the sorrow is too great,
If one can grieve for one's own suicide.

Faraway lands of calamity
Place names become scars.
Mărăşeşti,[10]
The Dardanelles,
Caporetto,[11]
Verdun,
Tutrakan,[12]
Douaumont.
You came from afar to die in these places.
So many of you did not even know they existed
And that they waited for you, to become your graves.
The miles you covered,
The seas you crossed,
To end up at the great feast of war.
Europe invited the entire world to its suicide
And in the end, killed all the guests.
Did the songs of sorrow of the mothers in Tonkin, Siam, or
    Madagascar reach the trenches of the Somme, on nights
    before battle?
Did the prayers from Mali, from Senegal, calm the faces of
    the fallen on the Chemin des Dames?

---

[10] Last major battle of the eastern front in 1917 between Romanians and Germans.

[11] Italian forces defeated by the German army, in 1917.

[12] Location of a battle in 1916 between Romanian and Bulgarian forces, ending in a Bulgarian victory.

No.
It was too far away.
And the very distance was proof of its absurdity,
Proof that none of those young men,
Come from so far away,
Ought to die for a Europe that had decided to set itself on
    fire.
What is left after four years of bloodletting?
Bones on plowed fields.
Rusting weapons.
Rudyard Kipling still seeking his son, somewhere outside
    Loos.
What is left?
Broken faces,
Torn souls,
A peace to sign,
And the fire eaters coming back again,
For they can never get enough.

Listen to Harold Nicolson,
An English diplomat at the Paris Conference,
A young man terrified by what has been imposed on
    Germany.
He's the one who refers to "fire-eaters"
For he sees it, and says it:
The treaty of Versailles is a humiliation
And we shall pay for it.
Why does the victor always make one move too many?
At Versailles, the fire-eaters are the ones who decide, who
    impose, who swagger,

Who set us up for the inevitable revenge.
What is left after four years of bloodletting?
Trees like toothpicks,
Fields full of screw pickets,
Shell holes, and three fallen empires.
The Ottoman, the Russian, and the Austro-Hungarian have
    fallen, and given Europe its new face.
But it has not had time to catch its breath.
Everything's going too quickly.
History never waits for us to be ready.
After this First World War,
Europe should have spent twenty or thirty years healing its
    wounds . . .
A decade of silence,
Devoted simply to memories of the dead,
And to reconstruction.
But the fever is there,
Europe has shadows under its eyes, and still it cannot sleep.

V
HURRY!

Is it time to be stunned?

Yes.

To dance, to smoke, to shout, to paint?

Yes.

Is it time to send the old world to hell, to descend into jazz
    cellars where time is immaterial,

To write poems in Paris cafés that will amaze the world?

Yes.

Is it time to say, "Never again," and live it, voraciously,
    resisting all the rest?

Yes.

We were too obedient.

For centuries,

And it just expanded the cemeteries.

Is it time to wave our arms, misbehave, and grin broadly
    with defiance?

Yes,

Please,

It's long overdue.

Europe needs Josephine Baker's breasts and Cendrars's
    poems.

Europe needs Brecht's cocky cabaret humor

And the painters from La Ruche.
Europe needs *Nadja*,[13]
To explore magnetic fields,
And cast its eyes upon the nudity of Man Ray's violin women.
Is it time to drink,
To be insubordinate?
Yes.
Die Goldenen Zwanziger,
The Roaring Twenties,
Come quick!
Make haste, and laugh,
Finish the bottles,
Let's have them, one after the other—paintings, books, poems,
Quickly!
Hurry, and run through the crazy streets of Paris and Berlin, feel their pulse.
Hurry up.
The night is noisy,
Not just with the sound of trumpets,
But with our own commotion.
Europe is learning to look inside itself
And it's frightening, bottomless, but intoxicating, too.
Dr. Freud is drawing his strange maps on his rug-covered sofa,
Maps that are labyrinths of desire, of repression, of drives and terrors.
Night stirs,

[13] 1928 novel by André Breton.

And we are inhabited.
Everything is swarming.
Hurry to *The Threepenny Opera* at the Theater am
    Schiffbauerdamm
To see Lotte Lenya and Kurt Weill.
Hurry to hang around what Henry Miller called "the navel
    of the world,"
The intersection of Raspail, Vavin, and Montparnasse,
Where so many feet have trodden.
So much doubt,
And exaltation,
And exhaustion.
So many coffees have been drunk,
There,
In those sidewalk cafés,
To avoid staring at one's famished solitude.
Hurry,
Already the insults are flying.
Already, politics reek of castor oil.
Already they're referring to men as "vermin,"
Red vermin,
Jewish vermin,
Sodomite vermin,
And on October 24, 1929,
It all comes crashing down.
Europe stops dancing:
The music from New York has suddenly stopped.
Black Thursday,
Then, Black Tuesday, even worse,
Then, black winter, you can't get up, now,

Then the great black decade
Causing nations to tremble.
Wheelbarrows of cash and ruined lives.
Europe is turned upside down.
Not from its wounds
But from the hemorrhaging of banknotes.
Everything grows tense,
Faces,
Speeches.
The lines of the unemployed grow longer.
Hurry and enjoy yourself some more,
If you still can,
But your heart's not in it anymore.
The intoxication didn't last.
And the political street has never been more violent,
In Germany,
In Italy,
Never so many fights, so much intimidation, fists flying and
    smashing faces in,
Never so many broken shop windows,
Offices ransacked,
And murders.
Because they've begun killing again.
In a targeted way:
Trade unionists,
Opponents,
Journalists,
Thinkers,
They're killing everything that looks like democracy and
    intelligence,

And Rome's getting used to it,
Berlin's getting used to it.
Almost one victim a day . . .
Matteotti, assassinated,
Walther Rathenau, assassinated.
The Rosselli brothers, assassinated.
So many more nameless in the face of History.
History is lighthearted,
It soon gets bored with these endless lists of victims.
It spreads its arms and moves ahead.
We can't remember all the names,
We just have to live with it.
The National Fascist Party,
That's what's coming.
It's happening so quickly.
The national socialist workers' party,
Singers of the outstretched arm,
In their gleaming uniforms
Faces turned to the Guide.
Oh, how good it feels to obey again.
What could be better than being in unison,
Marking time,
And scrapping with the enemy.

You smell it?
There's new odor everywhere in the streets of Berlin.
On May 10, 1933,
On the Opernplatz:
A bonfire of books.
Brecht, Döblin, Freud, Marx, Mann, Zweig,

Bücherverbrennung.

They'll do it nearly everywhere, mountains of scandalous papers.

Mountains of Jewish authors, pacifists, depraved, and corrupt,

Mountains burning nicely while the crowd salutes, arms outstretched.

Joseph Goebbels is there

      Spit on his name,

He's talking about "purification."

He's afraid that decadent culture might be contagious.

He's right about one thing: there's nothing more contagious than books.

So, do you smell it?

In Bonn, Bremen, Hanover, Frankfurt, Heidelberg, Nuremberg, Rostock, Hamburg,

Elated students tossing masterpieces onto the fire.

Oh, how good it feels, not to be an individual anymore.

To abdicate one's mind,

One's will,

To submit

Avidly,

Totally,

To the group,

Arms outstretched like the others,

To something better than a group,

To a leader.

Obedience

Will have been humanity's greatest concern.

To obey and to sing,

There's no better way to arrive at killing.

Everything is tension, irritation.
Pogroms,
Beatings.
*"Never, in all its existence, has the world been so globally
    irritated, so totally agitated."*[14]
He could feel it, Zweig, the tension pervading the cities.
Spreading along the roads.
The great murder is coming closer,
Has decided on its targets.
The *Münchener Post* is trying to count the casualties,
As best they can
To defy Hitler.
The paper survives for a decade,
Until the day the Brownshirts come swooping down on the
    offices to ransack them.
All the journalists are arrested and deported.
The *Münchener Post* will be an empty building from now
    on,
A mausoleum of melancholy
Foretelling a future of misery.

[14] *Die Schlaflose Welt*, Stefan Zweig.

VI
UNDESIRABLE

From so many towns, regions, countrysides, they have to
    flee.
So many men and women must try to find shelter.
Entire families leaving everything to get to France,
    Switzerland, England,
Or to make it to the United States.
As soon as they are on the road, they are given a new name:
"The Undesirables."
The continent becomes a complicated map: points of pas-
    sage, roadblocks, closed borders.

They leave Germany.
The Jews smell sulfur and hatred in the air on the
    Kurfürstendamm,
And leave in great haste.
They arrive in France,
Convinced they'll be welcomed as allies.
They have left everything,
In a few hours,
Their apartments,
Their professions,
Their families,

They have come here for shelter.
And they're stunned when they first hear their new name:
"Fritz."
Whether you're Jewish or not,
An opponent or not,
"Fritz," either way.
No distinction made.
Not an era for nuance.
They're German, and reviled in the streets of Paris,
And so
They're undesirable,
Yes.
German Jew is the name of misfortune
And to the very end the world will cast stones at them.

They are leaving Turkey.
The new state wants no more Greeks,
Nor does Greece want its Turks.
A population exchange on a grand scale.
The Great Catastrophe has struck the families in the east.
One and a half million Greeks leave Istanbul and the lands
    of Anatolia,
And fearfully discover the streets of Athens.
They arrive with their bundles and their fear, with the faces
    of the dispossessed.
They are told this is their country, but they know it's not
    that simple.
People mock their accents
And fear their numbers.
So old women open their suitcases,

Close their eyes,
And breathe deeply, searching one last time for the smell of
    the far shore.
Every night they listen close, openhearted, to the sad notes
    of *rebetika*,
Their only comfort.

They are leaving Spain.
Barcelona has fought, but will fall.
The men of the Durruti column,
The besieged Catalans,
POUM members, communists, anarchists, republicans,
All head for the Pyrenees.
The *Retirada* crosses the mountains
To end up in the sadness of the poverty of exile.
Camps on beaches fill with exhausted, filthy crowds.
They are safe and sound but they too discover their new
    name:
"Undesirable"
And must learn to bear it.

Europe begins to wander.
France welcomes three million foreigners in the 1930s.
"Welcome" is the wrong word.
France watches as three million foreigners arrive,
It doesn't welcome them.
Listen to Daladier:
"We have to get rid of the Undesirables."
Clearly stated, nothing flowery.
And so they're rounded up in camps.

Dozens of camps,
Small and large.
These crowds have to be controlled,
Their numbers checked, their destinations known.
"Concentration camps" are set up.
That's what they're called,
In Rieucros, in the Lozère
Not far from Mende.
The camp at Rivesaltes and the one in Les Milles.
All over France
Barbed wire will grow, like wild grass.

There is a Europe of the stateless.
Of those who flee,
Who leave in the night,
Entrusting their lives to smugglers,
And they pray they won't be sold at the end of the road.
There is a Europe of old rags,
Of tired mothers
Who know that countries can be traps, can snap shut
    again, violently.
There is a Europe of governments in exile.
London becomes the capital of resistance.
The governments of Belgium and Poland,
The kings of Norway, Greece, and Yugoslavia,
The queen of Holland,
Representatives of Free France,
Have all crossed the Channel.
An era of counterfeit passports.
The border reigns supreme

And takes millions of lives hostage.

For how many men and women has Europe been a land of
  suffering?

The Irish of the Great Famine

The Italians of the Mezzogiorno

The Jews fleeing everywhere . . .

For how many has Europe become unbearable?

Some find their way through the indescribable chaos.

Arthur Koestler, a Jewish child from Budapest, whose eyes
  do not mislead him.

Fred Uhlman, who manages to save himself

Because a friend taught him this phrase—as simple as an
  urgent call to leave everything behind:

"Il fait beau à Paris aujourd'hui."[15]

Brecht, who leaves for Denmark, Zweig for Brazil.

Some escape,

Others, staring out at a world on fire, cannot cast off their
  lethal melancholy.

Walter Benjamin makes it through occupied France

Only to commit suicide in Portbou, in his little hotel room.

As will Zweig, with his wife in Petrópolis.

The world is stifling

And it's not enough to elude hatred.

What if that word hanging over them

In the final moment,

Whispering and leering

"Undesirable"

[15] Title of an autobiographical novel by Fred Uhlman.

That word
Made them give up?

Everything is ready now.
Arrests in the middle of the night:
Yes, sir!
Calls to murder:
Yes, sir!
A huge crowd, marching:
Yes, sir!
The world has gone mad,
And does not sleep.
No more sleep
Only a fierce joy.
States go bankrupt:
Yes, sir!
Nights are long,
Days, too,
Weeks, months,
We cannot see the end of this long warpath ahead,
Yes, sir,
Yes, sir!

VII
IN RUINS

War has returned.
No longer digging the earth into trenches,
It's taken possession of the skies.
Every country carpets enemy territory with bombs.
The towns look so small from up there:
Checkerboards of cramped lives in black and white.
The century fills with the sound of Stukas,
Dive-bombing roads and destinies.
The towns set their clocks by the rhythm of the air raids.
The Reich advances,
Swallows land,
Multiplies its spoils of war,
Plants its flag on the Grand-Place in Brussels and at the
    Trocadéro.
Those who still resist are bombed.
Inhabitants must be terrorized, enemy morale broken.
Since Britain is the only country with its head held high, it
    suffers a concentrated onslaught of bombs."
Every day from now on
The airplanes will drop fire and death.
Every day,
They do battle in the anxious skies over Britain.

The East End is burning in a hell of tall, crackling
    flames.
Great Fire over London.
Great Fire again,
Like in 1666.
Everything is burning,
And people burrow underground in tube tunnels,
In shelters,
Basements,
Or under the table.
A torrential rain of bombs upon the city.
The young pilots of the Royal Air Force have no time now
    for drinks at the White Hart in Brasted,
They have to keep pace with combat,
Sometimes taking off six times a day,
And dying, often.
Every day goes by,
Every day expires,
But every day, Britain resists.
To shatter a nation's nerves,
Wear down its leaders through exhaustion,
That is the aim of the Blitz.
But they can't do it.
Because there is this voice,
Determined and calm,
That goes on encouraging the free world, tenaciously:
"We shall fight on the beaches,
We shall fight on the landing grounds,
We shall fight in the fields and in the streets,
We shall fight in the hills,

We shall never surrender."[16]

Every night,
For nine months,
Sirens wake families,
And bombs light the streets with their fiery glow.
Every night,
But London resists.

Many cities in Europe knew death from the sky.
Warsaw,
Guernica,
Rotterdam,
Belgrade.
A few minutes,
The time it took to fly overhead,
Bombs falling in heavy clusters.
At random, life, death,
At random, victim or survivor.
In Stalingrad,
An inconceivable deluge, causing more than forty thousand deaths in two hours.
There are many cities, suffering and dying.
Athens dies with its mouth agape.
Megalos limos.
They are dying of hunger in the shadow of the Parthenon, and the streets are lean.
And when it's Germany's turn to falter,

---

[16] Winston Churchill, June 4, 1940, House of Commons.

Punishment will come from the sky once more.
Cologne,
During the *Tausendbombernacht*,
Essen,
Berlin.
General Arthur Travers Harris, known as "Bomber Harris,"
    persuaded Churchill to raze the German capital to the
    ground:
The British bomb at night, the Yanks during the day.
Lübeck, Rostock, and Dresden are annihilated,
The cities are piles of rubble,
Of great collapsed carcasses,
Cathedrals in shards,
Vestiges of lives, apartments, avenues,
Razed to the ground,
Knees to the ground.

Nazi Germany had a dream of Europe:
A subjugated continent.
From Warsaw to Oslo,
Amsterdam to Vienna:
Plundering.
But oppression gives birth to the spirit of resistance.
Listen to Camus speaking to his enemies.
In the heart of the dark years, from the clandestine hours
    of combat, he says:
*"Ours is a joint adventure that we shall continue to pursue,
despite you, in the wind of intelligence."*[17]

[17] *Letters to a German Friend* by Albert Camus.

We have heroes who sketched the dream of a pluralistic
    Europe
That Camus would baptize with an obvious name:
"My greatest homeland."
They fought for that homeland.
Plunged their hands in the fire
And although they were only twenty,
They were solemn, as if saying farewell.
In a world of dishonest compromise
They used their lives as compasses.
Our countries twisted from inside.
Old men—once glorious—became lackeys to crime.
Complacent hands, signing acts of submission.
We needed young voices to hold our heads high again.
We were endowed with heroes:
Those who chose rebellion,
Sticking posters,
Little messengers,
Arms smugglers,
Scouts of hideouts.
We are endowed with heroes:
The Manouchian cell, which spoke with every accent but
    bled in French.
The *tajne komplety*, which set up underground schools so
    the Polish people could go on learning.
The Lingekompaniet in Norway.
Joachim Rønneberg who sabotaged Nazi Germany's
    nuclear program.
Irma Bandiera's Garibaldi brigade
With only one survivor remaining.

Andrée De Jongh's "Comet line" with her legacy of resist-
 ance,
The two Oversteegen sisters, Freddie and Truus, and their
 red-haired friend Hannie Schaft, who was executed in
 the dunes at Bloemendaal.
Young people learning to handle dynamite,
To lay ambushes,
To empty a gun in a restaurant,
And to die.
Young people learning the pain of impossible choices,
The vertigo of retaliation.
Did Rosario Bentivegna weep when he set off the bomb on
 the via Rasella?
When it killed thirty-three SS?
But in retaliation came the massacre at the Ardeatine
 caves, with three hundred and thirty-five civilians
 killed.
Heroism is painful,
It wearies the mind
With its ugly face of bloody choices.
We are endowed with heroes
Who rushed into chaos
To give birth to a greater homeland.
They fought back with all their vitality
Against those vociferators in shirtsleeves,
And those who march in time,
And little notables of collaboration,
And torture in cellars.
We are endowed with heroes
Who left us a continent more vast than all our countries,

A land where we must live
For them,
"In the wind of intelligence."

VIII
WIR, ASCHE

We know what it means to disappear,
We've lived through it so often:
The threat of barbarians,
Empires falling.
We know what it means to have reigned supreme,
And then fade away in the immensity of time.
Each of our countries has known enlightenment and ruin.
But there is something else,
Darker still:
Man's inhumanity to man.
Methodical killer,
Inventor of death at an industrial pace.
We know.
Here on this European land,
Optimism was killed
And that makes us
The inheritors of anguish.

When does it begin?
Horror penetrates in successive shifts.
First there are the speeches,
Electrified by the elation of hating out loud.

Speeches brandishing race as the only answer,
Gargling on the word,
"Race,"
To establish hierarchies.
They will found a concept of perfection,
And its corollary: the existence of an inferior category.
And so, overnight, there are Aryans, and the others.
The superior beings, and the others.
Lives that count for less, than the others.

When does it begin?
Is it when words become harsher?
When they start talking about "gangrene,"
"Vermin,"
"Parasites,"
And "cleansing?"
With eugenics?
Forced sterilization?
The race must be pure
And already their hands are learning to kill.

When does it begin?
With the vast crowds who come together and agree to for-
    swear thought,
Who let themselves to be claimed by fervor,
By the pleasure of chanting a name in unison,
And of walking in step,
Always the same,
The step toward alienation.

When does it begin?
With the *Kristallnacht*?
That night when hatred is unleashed like a baited dog.
Shop windows fall,
Synagogues burn.
It must go faster, the emigration of German Jews,
Or their deportation.
They are dragged into the street,
Their beards set on fire,
They are forced to kneel
Then beaten black and blue.
These are hours when criminal mockery meets with
    applause,
When calls for murder and gunfire meet with applause.
Perhaps that's what they're testing during the *Pogromnacht*:
The Nazis want to know if Germany is ready,
And it is.

When does it begin?
When they move the Jews and herd them into ghettos.
In Vilnius, Warsaw, Minsk, Lublin, Łódź, Kraków,
First, they gather them,
Then they lock them away.
In one day, the Warsaw ghetto becomes a prison
And the men, women, and children inside begin to die.
On the other side of the wall, people go about their shop-
    ping.
On the other side of the wall, they wear coats and eat
    chicken.

It has begun.
Jews are murdered on the roads.
Genocide by bullets,
In the beginning.
Ditches, all over Eastern Europe,
Dug by the very people about to be killed.
The result of decades of pogroms
Always singling out the same enemy,
In Russia, Poland, in Ukraine,
Always the same:
"The Jews,"
To whom everything can be done since they are less than
    nothing.

Immense heaps of shoes left behind,
And as they arrive at the camp, the sound of soldiers open-
    ing train doors.
Heaps of shorn hair,
Heaps of clothes,
Of suitcases,
Shoes,
Gold teeth,
Heaps of little things, bowls, pewter goblets,
Heaps left behind,
The moment they enter death.
Heaps
That is the moral of the story.
Heaps of bodies
To be shoveled up,
Heaps

Six million men, women, and children
Become
Heaps
That is what it is,
That we can neither
Say
Nor think.
Heaps
There is nothing
Left
Sie haben uns
Heaps
Zu Haufen
Gemacht.
And we stop at the abyss
We know all we can do is stay silent.

Man's inhumanity to man.
Infinite vertigo when confronted with obedience,
With the death wish.
Century of ashes,
Century suffocated by an unprecedented smell
That should never have existed,
A smell that burns the earth
And makes the fir trees weep.
Humans gassing other humans by endless shovelfuls.
Ashes.
That's all that's left.
Ashes
In huge mountains

How can we even believe it?
That this happened?
Ashes of
Lives
Scattered,
Then
Heaps
Of ashes
Heaps,
Von jetzt an
Nichts.

Trains came from all over Europe
Unloading at Auschwitz, Sobibór, Chełmno, Treblinka,
    Belsen.
Lives,
Stories,
Children.
Do you remember the railway?
The pride of the 19th century?
Do you remember *The Rocket*, from Manchester to
    Liverpool?
Railway tracks springing up everywhere,
Signs of progress,
Of modernity?
Those rails, all at once,
Have become the literal image of death.
The train, that was
Europe's pride and glory,
Becomes the emblem of its destruction.

A rail network in Europe that subsumed entire populations
    and gassed them.
There will be nothing left
At all
Nothing,
Überhaupt
Nichts.

Humanity has been vanquished.
Black hole,
Subsuming us all.
"Ashes" is the word of the anti-century
Not the ashes of the Bible,
Not the ashes of the cycle of creation,
Of existential humility,
No, the ashes of hatred.
"Ashes" is the word that stands against everything the 19th
    century believed in:
Progress,
The virtuous rhythms of machinery,
Humanism.
Ashes
And there is nothing more to say,
In this place,
Nothing more
Heaps of impossible
Words,
Nichts
Mehr.

So what is there to say?
For a long time,
Nothing.
What is there to say
For a long time
Think about that
Nothing
All the space it must take up
Nothing
So vast
So terrifying
And the silence
Nothing
Which alone captures the immensity
Of what we cannot name.
Nothing
Only
Memory.
That is all there is:
Preserve
The memory.

IX
THE GREAT RETURN

"Have you seen this face? . . . Please, take a moment to
    look at this photograph . . .
"Does he remind you of anyone? . . . Are you sure? . . . "

And now the great return,
The survivors of the concentration camps,
        An emaciated mass, a shocking vision,
Prisoners of war,
And all the displaced populations,
Those who fled,
Jewish children in hiding,
Families divided,
Imagine,
On the scale of an entire continent,
The great return.
The borders have shifted.
People want to go home
But home has changed countries.
And many are stateless.

"Have you seen this face? Please, take a look . . . "
The same question, asked in stations, hospitals, school-
    yards,

Everywhere,
With the same expectancy,
Always disappointed,
Always feverish.
Have you seen . . . ?

The homecoming
Takes time.
You cannot just walk through the door to your home the
    morning after the armistice.
Look at Primo Levi,
A living skeleton
As he starts on his long homeward path from Auschwitz to
    Turin,
By way of Ukraine, Byelorussia, Moldova, Romania,
    Hungary, Austria . . .
Eight long months of homecoming,
Across a ruined Europe,
Bridges destroyed,
Railway lines obstructed.
How do you get home?
What road do you take?
With what money?
Look at them, all the people rushing to the Grand Hôtel
    Lutetia in Paris,
For news.

"Have you seen him? It's my son, my brother . . . Does he
    look at all familiar to you? He lived here . . . I haven't
    heard anything. Please . . . No? Nothing? . . . Really?"

*

Every day,
The deported come home.
Families bring photographs from before the war,
To wave in the faces of survivors as they ask:
"Have you seen? . . . Please . . . It's my brother, my hus-
    band, my lover."
They don't realize.
That the face in the photograph means nothing
Because the man in the photograph is wearing a waistcoat,
    a hat,
And looks handsome,
With an elegant mustache.
The women in the photographs
Have long hair,
Combed,
Braided,
They're wearing blouses,
But those who survived the long hunger of the ovens
Were a multitude of shaven heads.
"Have you seen . . . "
Every day,
The impossible question,
Every day
They ask it again.

And on all the roads of Europe
Exhausted bodies
Breathe inaudibly,
Hoping to make it.

Jorge Semprun comes home,
Elie Wiesel, too.
Simone Veil and Marceline Loridan-Ivens come home,
Robert Antelme,
Charlotte Delbo,
Stéphane Hessel come home,
All these young people who survived
Come home,
Without their family.
They will have to take up their lives again
Without witnesses,
Without the kindly eyes of those they loved.
Some won't make it,
They'll die there,
On the trains, going home.
On the roads leading nowhere.
Too long,
Too hard,
Too exhausted.
They will die free, but do they know that?
Does it bring them any joy?
"Have you seen . . . She's my wife . . . my sister . . . my
    mother . . . "
So often, there's no answer.
So often, for so many dead.

Europe is gridlocked with lost shadows.
The Red Cross,
The French Popular Relief,
The Secretariat for Refugees

For survivors,
That's where they work,
De Gasperi,
Schuman,
The future fathers of European construction.
They have seen it, that Europe of the roads, the bundles,
    the thin bodies.
So many lost lives
Need a passport.
Hosts of people have no more nationality.
They need papers so they can lay down their burden of suf-
    fering.
So they can go home,
And breathe slowly,
Calmly,
And tell themselves,
In the silence of an attic room,
Tell themselves,
That they've survived.
That's all,
Survived.
Tell themselves
To make it true.

Who are our fathers?
The question this century keeps asking.
We must try to picture it,
In villages all over Europe,
Fathers going home,
After being prisoners,

Deported,
Or soldiers,
After fighting in faraway countries
Or staying hidden.
They knock at the door,
Bang their shoes against the wall, not to dirty the house
    with the filth of war,
And there are children there.
"This is your father," they are told.
"Aren't you glad to see your daddy?"
Eyes open wide
Looking
Not really daring.
They are three, or four, or five years old,
They've been raised by a mother who thought she was a
    widow,
And cannot believe she has a husband again.
She puts her arms around him, weeps, covers him with
    kisses,
But the children, no, they don't know what to do . . .
"This is your father."
Should they hold out their hand,
Or run into his arms?
Who is this old man,
Ragged,
With shadows in his eyes?
Who are our fathers?
For twenty, thirty years, young Germans will wonder . . .
Good family men,
Jovial,

Loving,
Making victory signs in photographs while wearing their SS
   uniforms.
An entire country of young men unsure of their lineage.
Suddenly their inheritance is quicksand.
At any moment,
Opening a desk drawer,
In the midst of a conversation,
They might find out that those who raised them, and loved
   them,
Are tainted with murder or evil deeds.
The present has been laid with traps
For decades.
An entire generation will grow up with this question,
Despicable when it has no answer:
Who are our fathers
And what gave birth to us?

X
Blocs

Slowly Europe senses it can cast off the Nazi yoke.
In Greece, Yugoslavia, Poland,
Everyone hopes for liberation, feels it, sees it, calls for it.
Cities are ready to raise their heads:
Paris rises up,
So does Warsaw.
The populations shout, push, yearn for victory,
But yesterday's allies are already looking at each other
    fiercely.
What is at stake now
It's not to beat the Germans anymore,
It's to beat them as quickly as possible.
Advance becomes the new order.
Faster,
Farther.
Occupy the terrain,
Drive home your advantage.
The era believed that surely the great challenge of their
    generation would be to count the dead, feed the living,
    and rebuild the country,
But they were wrong.
History never waits for us to get ready.

It has already moved on to something else.

Give me a month of your life,
And then another,
And then a third.
Give me a year of your life,
So I can push back your dreams and stifle your desires.

Oh yes, it is all going fast.
It is our turn to be carved up, fragmented, occupied.
Do you remember the Berlin Conference?
One for you,
One for me.
Do you remember?
"Any power can extend its domination inland until it meets
   a neighboring sphere of influence."
Times have changed, but the hunt continues.
They've swapped the pith helmet for the Katyusha.
No longer sailing up rivers in humid heat,
But pushing tanks along country roads as fast as they
   will go.
Must be quick,
Go ever farther.
Seize, while we can.
What's not yours can still be mine.
So Churchill meets Stalin
And on a scrap of paper, they countersign *the naughty doc-*
   ument
Which lays out the zones of influence:
Poland, in the USSR's pocket;

Romania, 90% for you and 10% for me.

Hungary, fifty-fifty;

Zones of influence, remember?

Czechoslovakia, yours.

And Yugoslavia, for you, provided you give me Greece.

Borders have moved again

And that's never a good thing.

"The farther we get from war, the more each side asserts itself," says Zhdanov.

Which also means:

The farther we get from war, the more we make ready for the next one.

The fire-eaters can tell they won't be getting their rations of shells, trenches, and bullets.

But they smile through it all,

For they know there are other ways to devour one another.

Done with battlefields.

And bombardments,

Territory seized, and seized again.

Done with troop movements,

And attacks.

Done with hot war, fast boiling flesh.

Ready for tension,

Escalation, provocation.

Ready for barbed wire and surveillance,

The elimination of opponents,

Fear.

Ready for repressed uprisings,

Gagged youth.
Ready for ordnance survey maps frozen in hostility.

How long does a war last?
Did World War II really end in 1945?
Ask the Greeks:
Their civil war is about to begin.
Ask the Poles:
For them everything is just ongoing . . .
A lead weight,
An iron curtain, and lives of silence.

My name is Władysław Bartoszewski and I wonder what life wants with me. At the moment, I'm only twenty-two years old. Does that seem young to you? No, I'm not young anymore. At the age of twenty-two, I have already been an inmate in Auschwitz-Birkenau, rescued thanks to the Red Cross. I am made out of the same stuff as nails. At the age of twenty-two I am a survivor, and I took up arms during the Warsaw insurgency. Paris, over there in the west, rose up. The victory was near but Warsaw didn't make it. The Germans got the upper hand again because the Russians did nothing. After the Katyn massacre, after the German-Soviet pact, this is what they did: they let the Germans crush us, within a hairbreadth of victory. And we lowered our heads, again. It's what they wanted. They knew they would get Poland and they didn't want a Poland full of heroes. They wanted destroyed souls. Life already seems long to me. Already I'm not at all young anymore, but it's not over. My name is Władysław

Bartoszewski and I'm not a communist. So it's prison
again, and fear again. For us there never was any victory.
Ever. The war lasted from 1939 to 1989. Fifty years. That's
a whole lifetime. My entire lifetime.

It's an era of impassable borders,
Barriers that are no longer raised.
Families will be cut off, severed, parted.
And it will last a long time.

Give me two years of your life so that you'll begin to doubt.
Give me five years for your children to be born under my
    rule.
Give me even more time
To leave you hopeless.

And yet, more than once, there are men who come along
Wearing the face of change.
Something's being born in Poland that seems to have
    momentum.
Gomułka is singing a new tune and the young people can
    breathe.
It's contagious, this youthful breathing,
So now Hungary opens its eyes wide.
On the square in Budapest where a statue of Sándor Petőfi
    stands proud,
The students are gathering.
There's a wave of excitement and Imre Nagy becomes the
    name of hope.
But it's too soon.

History doesn't want Hungarian freedom
History doesn't want Imre Nagy.
A rope is waiting for him in a Budapest prison
And they'll hang him there the way they hang all freedoms
    in the iron realm.

Give me two years of your life.
Three years, and your children.
Give me another year, two, four,
And that makes ten . . .
Give me ten more and that will make twenty.
Can anyone believe it will ever stop?

It's too soon.
The Cold War has only just begun.
Three hundred thousand Hungarians are fleeing from
    repression.
In Poland, Gomułka will betray his people and let the lead
    weight down again.
No freedom,
No,
History has other plans:
Impatiently awaiting the night of August 12, 1961.

Give me five years of your life while your parents die of old
    age,
And your children become students.
Give me two years and you'll have no more strength.
Give them, one after the other,
All your years,

There's no end to this hunger of mine.

In Berlin
That night
Comes,
And will leave the entire world aghast.
Almost fifteen thousand men of the armed forces of the
    German Democratic Republic block the streets
And put up fences and barbed wire.
The wall appears,
Cuts the city in two along a concrete line.
You can't cross over it
You can no longer meet.
Now you live so close, so far.
Two confounding rhythms of History.

Give me two years of your life and that makes so many
That I've lost count
And so have you.
Give me your whole life
And all the lives you dreamt of living.

When is a war over?
For a long time, Europe will live as half a body.
And Bartoszewski goes on talking
His gaze vacant,
Spitting on the History that stole everything from him.

My whole life. From the first day they bombed, on
September 1, 1939, when the Germans attacked Warsaw

and I woke up in the middle of the night, until 1989, my
whole life, stolen by war . . .

From now on, this will be a time for exiled dissidents,
Denunciations in hushed voices.
You must learn to survive in the Stasi's gaze,
Their ears,
Their hands.

Give me two more years,
Five more,
Give me everything, now.

Again and again
They'll put their lives in danger,
Take risks,
And struggle,
Again and again,
So that after fifty years,
At last,
They'll regain their freedom.
But the young fighters will be old men by then.
They won't dance,
Or embrace.
When victory finally comes,
They will only be able to weep.

XI
A Treaty for a Birth

"Never again."
So many generations said those words.
So many generations believed,
But that never prevents the desire for revenge and escalation, or the return of the worst imaginable.
Until one day a little group of men came up with a new way to say those words.
No more punishing the enemy, but becoming their ally.
And since the war was fed with steel and coal,
That is where we will begin.
The founding fathers—who don't yet have that name—
Crisscross the continent and try to win others over.
Never again.
We mustn't dominate Germany,
But bind its fate with our own.
No one had ever thought like this.
Who are these men who want to unite?
Monnet,
Adenauer,
Schuman,
De Gasperi,
Beyen,
Spaak,

Bech,
Over half of them have never been in office,
Neither tribunes nor politicians
But high-ranking civil servants,
Bureaucrats,
Men who've sat on commissions,
Used to international debate.
All born in the late nineteenth century,
They all lived through the two successive bloodbaths.
Some were imprisoned,
Many were in exile with their government in London.
Sometimes they knew the trials of flight and wandering:
They are men of borders.
They know what it means, in their flesh, to belong to several countries.
When he was born, De Gasperi was a citizen of the Austro-Hungarian empire,
Schuman was German.
The borders shifted beneath their feet
And De Gasperi became Italian,
Schuman French.
And so Europe, yes,
For a greater homeland.
"A day will come when all of you, nations of the continent, without losing your distinctive qualities and your glorious individuality, will be blended into a superior entity and you will constitute the European brotherhood."[18]
Victor Hugo gives words to faraway dreams:

[18] Speech by Victor Hugo at the Paris Peace Conference in 1849.

"The United States of Europe."
The European *"nation of nations,"*[19]
The reunion of wounded countries that embrace, so as not
    to go on tearing each other apart.

After Mussolini's fascism,
Hitler's National Socialism,
After the disgraceful regimes of Pétain in Vichy,
Vidkun Quisling in Norway
Anton Mussert in Holland,
Frits Clausen in Denmark,
Georgios Tsolakoglou in Greece,
Milan Nedić in Serbia,
Of Ante Pavelić and the Ustasha in Croatia,
After all that lot,
      Spit on all their names at once,
      They bear the same name
      Of servitude and connivance,
      Of hatred and anti-Jewish laws.
After all that lot,
Who will be judged,
Commit suicide,
Or end up in exile,
Europe needs to define herself as a social democratic polit-
    ical space,
A zone for deliberation and compromise.
The founding fathers are almost all Catholic,

[19] Expression used by Walt Whitman in "By Blue Ontario's Shore,"
to define the United States.

It's a Christian Europe,
Of the reasonable center,
Of political nuance,
And consensus.
A Europe of dignitaries,
And perhaps therein lies the original sin: the absence of the common people's passion.
But after the fury of war,
After the huge crowds drawn to one man with arms outstretched,
This was what was needed:
The calm atmosphere of shared debate.
How strange it is, this Europe.
This is not the way History plays midwife to countries or empires, as a rule . . .
There is always a revolution,
A conflagration,
The will of the people overthrowing everything.
In this case, no.
Europe was born without the crowds chanting its name in the street,
And that is new.
Europe was built without the enthusiasm of the people,
As a precaution,
Because the enthusiasm of the people led to crime.
Because passion in politics meant holding forth until the crowd turned fanatical.
Europe was built without resorting to direct suffrage, because it was emerging from a chaotic time when the people had got it wrong.

*

The European Coal and Steel Economic Community was
    born.
Then the Treaty of Rome was signed.
Look at the photographs that remain:
There's a long table,
With over fifty people standing around it,
In several rows.
We will get used to this:
Huge assemblies,
With signatures, handshaking, and cohorts of translators.
This will be our face from now on:
Long days of dialogue,
The endless signing of agreements,
Without passion,
Without getting carried away.
Nuance
And compromise.
Europe was born in reaction to what dogma and haste had
    produced.
So, yes,
In 1957,
A photograph immortalizing a long table where so many
    men we do not know are signing documents.
It looks like a huge board meeting
Or business gathering.
That is how we were born,
Because the ideological uprisings,
The so-called carnal bonds between a leader and his people,
Had led to suicide.

XII
BARE-BREASTED YOUTH

Hurry!
Come on! Come on! We need a lot of people!
Something's about to change, it's changing now!
Can't you feel it?
Young people are stirring, growing impatient, and now
    they're shouting:
Hurry up,
Come on, come on!
Their numbers are growing,
There's the thrill of being in a crowd
And they're taking possession of the streets:
Come on!
Hurry up!
Everything will be different now!
They're singing,
Laughing,
Making noise.
Listen to them,
Something rustling, rumbling, growing,
It seems to crack and split.
Some of them heard Dubček speak, that very morning,
And they're telling the others.

The leader said something about *"socialism with a human
    face"*
And the crowd feels dizzy:
It's practically a confession: the past didn't have a human
    face.
And so they believe in it,
They're meeting up,
Wandering around the streets together,
In a great outpouring of joy.

Woe to those who go too fast.
History doesn't like being shoved,
Or hurried along.
She's an ill-tempered old biddy, lashing out with her cane
    at anyone who rushes her.
She's obese,
An ogress,
Who likes for youth to serve her
And not the other way around.
Woe to those who get it wrong.
There are spring seasons that end in flames.
Socialism has hands,
And feet,
An entire body for crushing lives.
Eyes and ears
That spy,
Keep watch,
Shadow.
Czechoslovakia thought that Spring was coming,
Woe to those who get it wrong and cannot see the winter.

*

It's too soon.
The old ogress does not want to hurry her steps.
She balks,
Sniffs the air for a scent of blood
And she likes it.
Reactionary forces will win the day, not youth.
"Normalization" is on its way
And it sounds like tanks on cobblestones.
Back to the former stage,
Where socialism had no human face.
The Brezhnev doctrine:
"The weakening of any link in the international socialist system directly affects all the socialist countries."
No absences at roll call.
No shirking or breaking away.
If just one changes, they'll all be overthrown.
Run, young people,
Hurry up,
Come on, faster!
Run, to dodge the bullets!
The tanks are invading Prague
And there will be no Spring.
Wenceslas Square looks out at Czechoslovakia, which will suffer,
Looks at the young people, who will fall silent,
Looks at Dubček, who will know a long life of police harassment and surveillance.
A symbol in 1848, that square,
And now it is waiting

For Jan Palach to perish on its cobblestones.

I'm coming. Years later. I show up on the Square. I'm pale. If someone looked at me, they would notice, but right now no one is looking at me. My name is Jan Palach and I'm about to die. I have to concentrate. I know I'm deathly pale, but it doesn't matter. No one sees me. No one has noticed me because I'm young and no one can imagine that such a young man is about to burn like a torch. I walk once around the Square, protected by my youth. I don't look at the people I pass. I don't want to risk losing my nerve. My name is Jan Palach and in a few minutes, I will burn to wake up a nation, to get the attention of the entire world. I am going to burn to rattle the old tyrants, give them no reprieve, so that other young people will have a name to say during their nights of rebellion. Because there will be other nights of rebellion. Anger feeds off this: young people's bodies. So I'm giving my body. That's what I'm doing. My name is Jan Palach. I have nothing left to give my country but my death. And all those people walking by me, soon, they will know who I am, all those people who have never heard of me will know me. My name will be fire. My name will be anger. I'm pale, but I'll do it. I'm not thinking about anything anymore. I'm doing it, I'm saying goodbye to life, goodbye to pain, because I've decided to die.

Wenceslas Square sees the body catch fire,
Go up in flames before the stunned passersby,
Then turn to charred remains.

Wenceslas Square sees the body taken away,
The authorities posting policemen at every corner,
Fearful of spontaneous uprisings or other immolations,
Then the "return to a state of calm,"
Which means the population gagged, again,
The return to boredom,
To fear.
"Submission" becomes the name of every day.
They will wait twenty years for Spring to return,
Twenty years for the old biddy to stoop to change.
Wenceslas Square is waiting,
Knowing one day it will see
Václav Havel greeting the crowd
And next to him, old Dubček.
Brought out of his narrow cupboard of a life.
Oh, but it's a long time, twenty years,
It takes so long to wait for History.
People grow old,
And lives go by.

So close,
So far away.
Prague and Paris.
That same year,
With the same words uttered:
Come on,
Hurry up,
We need a lot of people!
Prague and Paris,
The same youth

But on one side, crushed, on the other, joyous.
On one side, authority clamps down,
On the other, a burst of mayhem.
That same year the Latin Quarter becomes a noisy lecture
    hall
Where chairs and desks are overturned
And cobblestones weigh less than slogans.
Europe discovers a young population
Who do not want to show respect,
Who do not want to wait their turn to speak,
Who do not want to take their place in Daddy's world,
Who want to upset everything,
Even heroes.
Barricades, again, crisscross the streets of the capital.
Paris, once again, full of invention,
Paris, surprising, again,
And beguiling.

Fuck your old rules and good manners!
Fuck the paterfamilias with his paper at dinner,
And the commands,
All the commands:
"Sit up straight,"
"Young ladies from good families don't say that sort of thing!"
Fuck the old order you imposed on us!
Fuck the road all laid out: loving spouse, exhausted
    mother, scorned wife!
Fuck boredom and a life in obscurity!
Fuck obedience and bras!
And orders to be good and polite and loving.

Fuck the bourgeois suffocation of so many lives!
We want our bodies
For pleasure,
For weeping,
For caressing.
Our bodies
To be alive,
Live life to the fullest,
With a big smile
And rapture in our gaze!

What is being born now
Is no small thing.
Paris becomes the center of a joyful uprising,
Lighthearted,
Throwing cobblestones
And making faces.
What is being born now,
Is the frenzied protest against the consumerism
Of our all-consuming societies,
The alienation of people who've become machines to pro-
    duce
Machines to consume
Machines to run.
Anger expanding against hollow lives:
Savings accounts and prosperity,
Little cardigans and woolen socks,
You must be reasonable, plan for the future, put money
    aside.
There is an age for getting good grades at school,

An age for choosing a loving spouse,
An age for taking your first steps into the real world, and
    an age for joining the Board of Directors . . .
Postwar boom and little deals on the side.
Triumphant middle class.
Fridge, washing machine, Christian democracy with a but-
    toned-up waistcoat!
Fortunately, there is this simple little phrase: "Don't waste
    your life making a living."
This might be enough:
It gets into your head and methodically chips away at you.
Lives lost to polite work.
An entire existence of ordered uselessness.
That's not life—life is kissing, running, suffering, embrac-
    ing!
Wanting what's new, relentlessly.
Intensity!
Intensity!

These days, sons want the truth from their fathers,
In Germany,
In Italy.
Sons have asked forbidden questions,
Voiced their rage at being children of silence.
What reemerges with May '68,
Is the Europe of momentum,
Mutinous,
Mischievous,
Allowing one to dream again.
May '68 bared its breasts to the old statues

And that fruitful gesture can't be measured in terms of
    political expediency.
People were happy just being people.
Happy to be young.
May '68 showed its breasts to the entire world.
Do not say it was a failed revolution,
It was something much greater,
The living reminding the political world that, without life,
    nothing can be achieved.
Young people are dancing,
Because they know they have won.
They are dancing
The way they will always dance
When they feel
They are a living statue of liberty.

XIII
THE WALTZ OF THE OLD GENERALS

Would you like to dance? No?

The old generals don't like the songs.
They look down on them
And that's their gravest mistake.
Because a song always brings them down.
But they won't believe it,
Nothing will convince them.
They've been warned, however,
People have brought them photographs and recordings.
They look at the singers,
Find them dirty, grotesque, effeminate.
They declare confidently that those rich kids will piss their
    pants the moment they send the security police for
    them.
How can the Greek colonels possibly understand Mikis
    Theodorakis and Maria Farantouri?
All they saw was a young woman with long hair,
And they were wrong.
The song "To Yelasto Pedi" will bring down their regime.

It's always a song that makes cracks in the walls.

On April 25, 1974,
At fifteen minutes past midnight
On Radio Renascença
They play *Grândola, Vila Morena*
By Zeca Afonso
—A song forbidden by the Salazar regime.
At a quarter past midnight
That song,
To all the officers in all the barracks
Is the signal they've been waiting for:
It's the order to go out and take possession of the city.
Marcelo Caetano takes refuge in the barracks on the Largo
    do Carmo
Stunned by what is happening.
The pace quickens when the people all sing the same song,
Afonso's song comes down from the Bairro Alto
Goes up to the Alfama,
Spreads all over Portugal.
The old generals are never wary enough of the songs.
They forbid them on the national radio,
Thinking that will be enough.
And if anyone dares speak about those songs again,
They'll exile the singers
But that doesn't stop Lluís Llach from composing *L'Estaca*.
"Si jo l'estiro fort per aquí
I tu l'estires fort per allà
Segur que tomba, tomba, tomba
I ens podrem alliberar."
Pull this way,
Pull that way,

That's what the people of the Mediterranean do.
Portugal,
Spain,
Greece.
Tomba, tomba, tomba . . .
The old generals cannot believe their eyes.
Unkempt young people,
Boys dressed like girls,
Girls showing their legs
Are defying them, singing, no longer afraid.
Tomba, tomba, tomba . . .
The songs spread from one country to the next,
Nothing stops them.
Jaruzelski, surely, never heard of Lluís Llach
Until the day a close counselor came into his office, looking contrite,
To have a word about Jacek Kaczmarski
And that song: *Mury*,
Which has inflamed the Solidarity strikers.
It's Lluís Llach's song,
Translated into Polish.
A song of walls, and stakes, and everything that must be toppled.
And suddenly the songs are on everyone's lips, in every street,
In Catalan,
In Polish,
Runa, runa, runa . . .
Nothing can stop them now.
A unified call to crack open:

If you pull here,
And I pull there,
If we all pull together,
Whether it's Franco
Or Jaruzelski,
They will fall.
Don't wait for them to die,
Generals live to a ripe old age.
They feed off the bodies that they have broken,
Look at Franco: eighty-three years old,
Salazar: eighty-one,
Jaruzelski: ninety-one,
The four Greek colonels,
Makarezos: ninety, Papadopoulos: eighty, Ioannidis:
    eighty-seven, and Pattakos: a hundred and three.
Don't wait for them to die,
Make them fall!
        Spit on their names and their old bones,
The songs are stronger than anything.
        Spit,
With the beautiful smile of youth.
Sing,
In the streets,
The cafés,
Sing the victory of your numbers.
The dead sing with you.
Those killed in brutal jails enter your voices
To sing with you
And bring everything toppling down.
Weep,

Dance,
Rejoice, people,
The generals fall,
And now your songs of struggle are hymns of freedom.

XIV
JOY, INDIFFERENCE

Now, joy.

It's there, pushing with all its might.

Europe has thrown out its fascist patriarchies.

But the regimes in the East are still in place.

Solidarity is getting busy,

Swelling its ranks.

Gdánsk defies the government.

Thousands of shipyard workers come out against the regime.

They aren't Prague Spring students, whom the government could scorn and call "petty bourgeois,"

These men are the very heart of the regime:

The workers.

The government is so old,

They've been there for so long,

Strengthened by all their schemes,

Complicit in so many murders.

Who can believe the regime will fall?

No one can, until it does fall.

No one can, until the last minute.

And when it does fall,

We still cannot believe it.

Only an hour ago
There was fear of police repression.
Then all of a sudden,
On November 9, 1989,
Everything falls and is turned upside down.
Young people scale the wall which, only yesterday, instilled
    such fear,
They sit astride it,
Bang on it with anything they can find . . .
Is this even possible?
No one dead for what they've done?
No one imprisoned for this banging,
With a hammer, a shovel, a mallet,
Or simply the palms of their hands?
Oh, how astonishing, this end of a regime so long feared,
So long crouching in the shadows to spy on you,
Denounce you.
Oh, the surprise of its sudden impotence.
Listen to the emptiness.
The barracks echo with the sound of absence.
The palaces, once inaccessible, are vacant now.
The clamor of the people is rising, everywhere.
From Prague to Berlin,
From Bucharest to Warsaw . . .
Everyone they feared,
The Honeckers, Jaruzelskis, Ceauşescus,
      Spit on their names,
All those who seemed so great
Suddenly become so small,
Unrecognizable,

Almost pathetic.
You can see it in their faces,
In their contrite expressions,
It emboldens the people in the street:
The generals are old,
Their time has passed.

Joy never lasts long in History,
No serene pause to catch one's breath.
Everything happens so quickly.
The tyrants fall
And in the collapse of their palaces we can already hear the
    rumbling of tomorrow's conflicts.
Freedom, sometimes, gives birth to war,
And joy, to indifference.
No sooner has the wall come down
Than a new conflict arises,
So near,
So soon.
The first war on European soil since the Second World War
With the name of a country that no longer exists,
That will give birth to six independent states:
Yugoslavia.
Everything goes up in flames.
War, again.
They say it,
Write it,
Repeat it on the evening news:
"Two hours by plane from Paris, people are killing each
    other,"

But Europe doesn't want to know.
Indifference has numbed people's minds.
They repeat the word "Balkans,"
To mean a natural powder keg,
Explosive by birth,
Engulfing anyone who meddles.
So Europe does what she does best: she doesn't move, she
    talks, holds meetings, legislates.
Leaves Izetbegović to shout himself hoarse, begging for
    weapons.
Men arrive on the scene with the familiar smug faces of killers:
Milošević,
Karadžić,
Mladić,
        Spit on their names,
Theoreticians of territorial partition,
And ethnic cleansing.
Already?
So soon?
Did we not say, "Never again?"
Yes, but the camps are there
With their emaciated bodies,
So we have to say it:
Yes, again.
So soon, after the joy.
Villages wiped off the map as soon as they've been
    "cleansed."
Blood, again.
Ditches dug at the edge of the forest,
Where at dawn they throw

The civilians they've killed
And violated,
And killed again . . .
Yes, again.
War
In Europe.
Yet it was only yesterday.
And what do people do?
Nothing.
Srebrenica dies,
Sarajevo dies
And we discover
The immensity of our indifference.

Europe is very good at hesitating.
Ugly face,
Comfortable impotence.
We know it well, that desire not to act.
It is there, inside us,
Feeding on our numbers,
On the complexity of the world,
Pandering to our comfort.
It is there,
Day and night,
It is our closest enemy.
Indifference seizing hold of tired nations
Draining them, diminishing them . . .
What can Europe do against the fatigue of its own nations?
As long as the continent trembled with war and submission,

Citizens wanted peace.
Today, they have it,
And they're bored with parliamentary democracy.
They want a leader, a strongman . . .
Yet where do leaders get you?
We know where.
We ought—more than anyone—to be wary of a population
    spellbound by the presence of a charismatic strongman.
But what can Europe do against voluntary servitude?
What can Europe do against us,
Or without us?

XV
ENLARGEMENT

The territory's vast and we don't know each other.
We have an entire continent to invent.
The fall of the Berlin wall opened two great expanses,
Amazed that they can now walk forward and embrace.
You say this enlargement has been too sudden?
That membership should have been more gradual?
But how could that have been possible?
To tell our long-lost brothers: "Wait . . . "?
To tell lives emerging from forty years of fear: "Patience?"
In 1989,
Europe smiled, broad-faced,
Proud,
In a way it had never known.

The territory's vast
And we don't know each other.
We have to explore it all, feel European through miles traveled.
Look at our great land.
The Europe of birches and olive trees,
The Europe of cathedrals and temples.
In the north, bricks,
In the south, whitewash,

Figs and blueberries,
Everything is vast,
And we are side by side,
Countries of beer, countries of wine,
Tea and coffee,
Cows and goats,
Spilliaert's light,
And Etruscan red.
The Europe turned toward the Atlantic,
Or gazing toward Istanbul,
We are all of that.
The territory's vast and we don't know each other.
We have no common language,
We are mosaics of lights.
From the ashy gray of the northern lands to the sun-struck
    Mediterranean whiteness.
Irish rain, Andalusian sierras,
From Dutch polders to Sicily's Monte Pellegrino,
We are an explosion of colors, accents, and stories.

Who are we now?
A nation of nations, vast and different,
Searching for a common ground on which to unite.
Are we Christian?
Is that what defines us?
No.
What best characterizes Europe is not Christianity itself,
    but its evolution over time:
How it's gone from an all-powerful religion to intimate
    worship, forfeiting power,

Allowing the coexistence of those who believe and those
    who do not.
Who are we now?
Children of dark hours,
But of irreverence, too.
There is the freedom not to believe,
To live free,
As free as possible,
In other words, to be prisoner to one's only torment,
One's own desires.
The freedom to love churches without loving religions,
To hold that the latter have brought humanity more blood
    than comfort,
More humiliating constraints than spiritual wealth.
The freedom to create one's own ethics,
An inner compass that is the choice, replayed at every
    moment, of what makes us human, what makes us wor-
    thy, or not, great, or not.
Too many St. Bartholomew's Days,
Too many Thirty Years' Wars,
Too much blood spilled,
Barns burned,
Bonfires where we've sent books, ideas, and heretics to die,
Too many lives walled up in convention,
Yearnings forbidden,
Longings constrained.
So, no,
Any characteristic held by a majority is not a defining ele-
    ment,
Otherwise we would be:

White,
Christian,
And old.
We are the children of a religious space that has so often
     torn itself apart,
Known so much internal strife,
That lost its ground and left the field of political omnipo-
     tence,
And that is good.
We are the children of its retreat,
Of coexistence with others,
And above all,
Of the option to "be nothing."
You can hear their consternation when they ask the ques-
     tion, somewhat apologetically, too polite to be shocked,
     but deep down they're sorry: "Really, honestly, you're
     nothing?"
Neither Protestant,
Nor Catholic
Nor Orthodox,
No, nothing,
Nothing other
Than humanist.

Who are we now?
What we share,
Is from having been through hell together,
Having been, each one of us,
Torturer and victim,
Gagged youth and blood-covered hands.

What we share,
Is a troubled humanism.
We know man's inhumanity to man,
We know the abyss,
We have been swallowed by its depth.
What binds us together, is that we are an anxious people,
Who know the shadow within.
Europe is a geography seeking to become philosophy.
A past that wants to be a compass.
A territory of five hundred million inhabitants,
That decided to abolish capital punishment,
To defend individual freedoms,
To proclaim the right to love who we want,
To be free to believe or not to believe.
We are humanists and that must be reflected in our
    choices.
No one God in Europe,
No pantheon to whom we must kneel.
The territory's vast and must remain so.
We have built a Babel continent,
Strange and complicated,
That only holds together thanks to this subtle balance
Between independence and brotherhood.

XVI
THE GREAT BANQUET

"Every generation, in relative opacity, must discover its mission, then fulfill it or betray it."[20]

Have we forgotten the words of Frantz Fanon?

Have we forgotten that in the eyes of History we are a generation?

That in the eyes of History we shall be judged for our courage or our failures?

Have we forgotten that we are not merely a crowd of individuals bound for happiness,

But an entity that must enlighten its era with new ideas?

Are we afraid of the word "mission?"

We find it overwhelming,

But rejecting it won't make it go away.

Rejection is simply the decision to betray it.

A great banquet.

That's what we need, now.

Passion,

Flesh, and words!

[20] *The Wretched of the Earth* by Frantz Fanon.

A great banquet,
Come,
Come one, come all,
Bring what is needed for revelry and debate.
Here it is, our mission:
Bring all the nations back to the heart of Europe.
Invite utopia and anger,
For nothing comes without them.
For too long Europe has stayed away from the noisy body
    of the people.
Afraid of their bad mood,
That they might fly into a rage,
For too long it lived with collective alienation.
It tried to invent an entity born of reason,
But in so doing, it forgot its lifeblood,
And saw the risk of becoming a great empty body.
Come on,
Over here,
A great banquet!
We have to get back to the passion of nations.
It won't be easy
Or sweet.
Nations progress in fits and starts, and overturn tables,
But Europe will die if it shuns passion.

Go on,
Hurry up.
A great banquet
Is our mission:
Something better than castrating administration.

Down with prescriptive decrees and standardization,
We deserve greater dreams.
Go on,
Come closer.
At the great banquet of nations, we must express our anger.
Anger, I say, when I see the European underclass,
And slow impoverishment in the shadow of comfort.
Europe cannot sit back and become a Hanseatic guild of
    great prosperous cities,
Exchanging their goods and their wealth.
Entire regions have been abandoned,
Kept apart from any new advances.
What is Europe to them, beyond just another name for
    scorn?
Every smile of modernity is a leering grimace.
Europe will only have meaning if it takes care of those
    who've been worn down.

Anger, I say, when I see how people scorn the vote,
Sometimes they've said no,
Sometimes they've rejected every suggestion,
Had their opinion scorned.
A lying plebiscite,
Tricking the voice of the ballot box.
Oh, democratic outrage violating the expression of refusal.
Little deals on the side, in the rear courtyard,
Where the nation thinks it will wrap up a shiny neat package,
Then cuts its fingers
And forfeits all legitimacy for years to come.

Anger, I say, when I see the Europe that cannot come up
    with an immigration policy.
Refugees are dying in the Mediterranean
Because our land makes them dream.
They climb into fragile crafts
Prepared to lose everything,
And we are wary of them . . .
Uncomfortable, we look at them,
Close our harbors,
Try to get rid of them.
Anger, I say, when I see the petty selfishness of nations
Who conspire to set their quota of men and women,
But some don't want any,
They balk,
Won't hear it, slam the door.
Others negotiate, every inch of the way, trying to make
    their own share lower . . .
Why are we so afraid?
There are five hundred million of us Europeans,
And does this number never seem to give us strength?
Are we so fragile?
To feel better, all we have to do is look deep in the refugees'
    eyes.
There, Europe is a powerful land,
Which protects,
And offers the promise of a chosen life.

The great banquet
It's time now
To bring forth all your ideas

And share them out.
The great banquet, in an uproar,
Of distortion.
It's time to shake things up,
So partisans of easy hatred lose the day.
It's time to invent.
We want a zone with limits to growth.
Do you remember overheating?
Gee up, mare-machine!
Faster! Harder!
We know where rampant competition and frenzied
    appetites lead.
We can become the greatest zone of steady economy.
The planet is dying from our appetite.
Dying from our desire to dig ever deeper.
Oil wells,
Shale oil,
Opencast mines,
Fossil fuels running dry.
We can invent something else besides bare-chested free
    enterprise,
Showing off its muscles.

More,
Come on,
Come one, come all,
And speak of utopia!
We want our nation of nations to have a new goal:
Not one of world domination.
In the days when we were empires,

We reigned supreme,
With haughtiness
And savagery,
Draining wealth and populations.
We were as ugly as those who reign today.
And then we died.
Empires crumble, erode, disappear.
We know what an eclipse is.
So many times, we died.
Ruling,
Then vanishing . . .
Ruling,
Then vanishing . . .
Is there a lesson to be learned from these disappearances?

But there are still proletarian states.
Will our progress mean their exploitation, once again?
Do we only know how to live to the rhythm of cyclical
    domination, as it varies with the waltz of raw materials?
Is that our plan: to dominate? Which means to subju-
    gate . . .
We have greater dreams than that,
We want to establish a balance in our relations
That won't be one of veiled exploitation,
That won't serve, like a thousand times before, to trample
    on
Humiliated populations.

Come,
Hurry up,

Uproar and utopia,
Bring everything with you.
Let Europe once again be the business of its people.
It will be a happy time.
Come closer,
Turn up the heat,
Ramp up the pace.
Like in the beginning,
But not from the steam of sweat, this time,
No, with passion and ideas.
Turn up the heat, ramp up the pace.
That's what we want:
For passion to return.
For Europe to come alive,
To change,
And to be,
Once again,
For the entire world,
The luminous face
Of audacity,
Spirit,
And freedom.